The Beginner Real Estate Investor's Guide to Your First Rental Properties

Gary Richards

© Copyright 2018-2019 Gary Richards. All Rights Reserved

CONTENTS

INTRODUCTION 4

CHAPTER 2: THE BASICS OF REAL ESTATE INVESTING 15

    The Two Big Ways To Make Money 16

    How to Begin 21

    Rural Markets 33

    Urban Markets 38

    Suburban Markets 44

    Single-Family Real Estate Investing 48

    Multi-Family Real Estate Investing 51

    Property Management Companies 55

CHAPTER 3: IN-DEPTH STRATEGIES FOR RENTAL REAL ESTATE INVESTING 59

    Tips and Tricks For Real Estate Investing 64

    Tools At Your Disposal 78

CHAPTER 4: YOUR PEOPLE AND ACCOUNTS 86

    Managing Your Finances 91

CHAPTER 5: ALTERNATIVE WAYS TO INVEST & CONCLUSION 100

    Creative Funding & Loans 106

CONCLUSION 115

GLOSSARY 118

INTRODUCTION

Have you ever looked at how rich people make money? Many seem to think that they earn their way through a large income with a lot of zero's at the end. However, reality is a bit different. While many of them surely worked hard for many years to achieve this status, by and large, their wealth does not stem from an 'income' at a company. Rather, it's what they do with their money that counts the most. Receiving your paycheck on Friday and then spending it all on perishable items before Saturday is over will guarantee that you'll never progress in wealth management. By the same token, stashing away your paycheck under your bed will not ensure that your savings will work for you in the long term. This book is designed to show how people can invest their money in real estate so that they do not fall into the same financial trap of their forefathers. In this work there are multiple tips and tricks into investing your money in real estate that may valuable income for you in the long run.

This book will have several parts to ensure that you get a holistic perspective of investing in real estate, along with the pros and cons involved in such investing practices. The next chapter of this book will discuss the basics to bring you up to date on rental property investing. This section will teach you how to buy properties in different types of markets, ranging from urban markets to rural ones. It also expands on the types of rental properties that are available for future investments (not all rental properties are created the same). *Chapter 3* will show you how to create a long-term strategy designed to secure profits over time. This chapter will also include certain tips and tricks that you can use as a first time investor. This chapter also illustrates the tools you will have as a first time investor that are designed to diversify your portfolio over time. The next chapter involves the community you create around yourself. While you may initially believe that real estate investing is a loner's game, in reality, you will likely be working with dozens of tenants, management companies, landlords, and others. This chapter also discusses back end issues, such as managing expenses, tabulating accounting information, and maximizing cash flow.

As with any new endeavor, you will make mistakes. *Chapter 5* will discuss some common mistakes new investors and landlords make. Ideally, when reading this chapter, you will hopefully not repeat some of these more common mistakes. This chapter will also discuss what your biggest liabilities are when you are renting properties. Finally, the last chapter of this book discusses alternative ways to invest in the real estate market. This section largely touches upon **exchange-traded funds** (ETF) and how you can invest in companies that handle real estate transactions and construction for rental properties. We will have some concluding remarks and a glossary for your convenience in this section as well.

For your convenience, all of the words that are in bold throughout this work will be defined in the glossary.

Before we begin discussing how you should invest in real estate, it is important to answer the question *why* should you favor this method of investment over others, such as putting your money in the stock market or hopping on the Bitcoin bubble. There are several pros and cons to investing in real estate over other options, but below are some of the straight facts. What all of these options have in common is that they are all forms of **passive income** (also known as passive investing). This type of income refers to cash flow that is managed by little to no effort – it is pretty much automated. Passive income, as the name suggests, is very different from **active income**, which is any income that you physically have to work for, such as in a job. Investing in the stock market or real estate is considered passive income because you are earning income from your investments, rather than producing a final result for a company. Now that we have this background knowledge on passive income, let's take a look at the two large types of passive income: the stock market and real estate investing.

First, there is no doubt which option is more lucrative in the long-term. The stock market has over-performed the housing market over the past thirty years. Below is a chart detailing the differences between the stock market and the real estate market.

Figure 1: Difference between stock market and real estate market (Source: S&P Dow Jones Indices)[1]

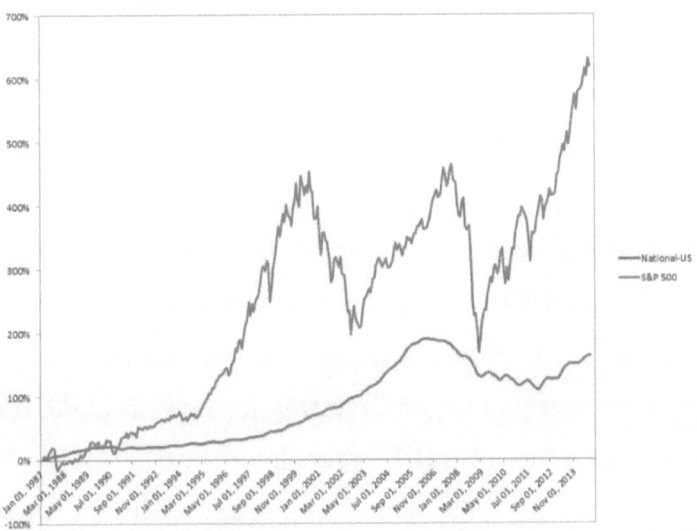

When looking at the chart above, we see two lines. The blue line is average the S&P 500 stock holding, while the red line indicates the average value of real estate properties. As we can clearly see, the stock market outperformed the real estate market over the past thirty years. If we were writing this book in 1987 knowing of such striking differences in performance, we would suggest putting your money in the stock market rather than in real estate. But let's take a look at the middle part of the chart to see if investing in the stock market would make sense. From the years

---

[1] Information on this chart can be found at https://www.cnbc.com/2014/12/08/where-to-put-your-cash-a-house-or-a-stock.html.

2000 to 2012, the stock market peaked and then dropped after the 9/11 attacks and subsequent War in Iraq. Then from 2004 to 2008, the stock market returned to its previous strength.

However, during the stock market crash of 2008 and the ensuing 'Great Recession,' the stock market line precipitously dropped yet again. The recovery took nearly seven years, but the stock market bounced back up again. If you were investing in the stock market in 1980, then there is a significant chance that you gained a substantial amount of passive income over the past 40 years. However, if you began investing in the year 2000, then you are not seeing returns until 15 years later. Furthermore, if you're looking to retire in 2009, then you just saw half of your savings disappear within a few months.

Now let's take a look at the red line. Clearly, this shows a much more conservative approach. The gains are not as large, yet the losses are negligible. From 1990 to 2008, the real estate market slowly and steadily increased in value. This means that if you are looking to buy and sell homes, you will likely see a steady increase in income over that 18-year period. Now let's take a look at the real estate market from 2008 to the present day. Remember how analysts were saying that it was sub-prime loans that caused the Great Recession? It's true, but it did not nearly influence the real estate market anywhere near as much as it influenced the stock market. From 2008 to 2012, we see a small slump in the real estate market, yet a huge drop in the stock market. Since 2012, the red line has again continued to increase. When looking at the two lines together, we notice that there are essentially two bubbles with the blue line. As a side note, stock market 'bubbles' appear as big spikes up in the value of the stock followed by a sharp decline. While the stock market experienced two of these spikes, the real estate market had some slow and steady growth over time, with only a minimal drop after the 2008 financial crisis.

So why did the real estate market only slightly dip during the Great Recession when the stock market pretty much crashed? The answer lies in cash flow. When there is a dip in the stock market, your asset is immediately lost. There is little anyone can do to change such a scenario. However, because the real estate market is physical (in the tangible sense that you can live in a home but not in the stock market), there is built-in value into those properties. This may come in the form of home improvement projects in upholstery, electrical wiring built into the house, new carpets, upgraded kitchens, enlarged bathrooms, and so on. Furthermore, if you have tenants living in your rental properties, they still have to pay rent. This means that your cash flow is still coming in despite the economic downturn.

Take your pick with these two types of passive income, but for this author, the slow and steady growth of the real estate market far outstrips the erratic changes in the stock market. If you are planning for the future, it's always better to have a secure and steady passive income than watching your money double and then drop by half, just to double again. If you do not read any further, make sure to understand this point: living off of your passive investments requires a steady and *predictable* increase, not an inconsistent doubling and halving of your savings. You will go from millionaire to pauper and back, not to mention the emotional roller coaster involved. This is especially true if you have a family and are interested in raising your kids in an emotionally stable environment.

There is a subtler advantage to investing in real estate over the stock market. You cannot live in your stock portfolio, but you can live in one of your properties. Investing your savings in the stock market may be more lucrative over time, yet if you are paying rent in an apartment or home, then the **opportunity cost** (what you could be doing with your money) outweighs the potential benefits. It is likely that the first property you buy will be the one that you live in. From here, then you can begin expanding your empire. However, it makes little sense to buy properties and renting them out to tenants if you are paying rent yourself.

Here's another pro to investing in real estate: ever heard of someone ripping you off when investing in a home? Probably not. If you do your homework, you should be able to tell if a property is a worthwhile investment. Barring extreme situations (such as a hurricane or an earthquake destroying your property), you can tell if a property's value will increase over time. Now let's take a look at the stock market. People get ripped off investing in the wrong stocks every single day. Bad advice, crooked fund managers, bloggers depicting stocks that are "guaranteed to go up," and authors interested in selling books are all taking advantage of the volatility of the stock market. This is rarely the case with real estate properties.

Because the rules of the game are different for real estate investing, it is difficult for an advertisement, book, or blog to direct you in the wrong direction (provided you do some homework, of course). While defrauding people may be the name of the game in selling some books or ideas in the stock market, this is not the case in the real estate market. There is a further, and more dangerous point to be made here: there are no **bots** (short for robots) in real estate investing. Bots essentially use complex algorithms and sophisticated modeling to buy and sell investors' equities, thereby influencing stock market prices. This adds an extra layer of complexity to investing in the stock market that does not exist in real estate investing.

Just as there are multiple positive aspects to buying homes and rental properties, there are some cons that should be taken into account. Stocks, by and large, are not subject to property taxes. There are so-called **capital gains taxes** (CGT) that the investor has to account for, but these are not as variable as property taxes. CGTs are taxes realized from the sale of your stocks. For example, let's imagine that Bill in Washington buys 100 shares of a stock at $5.00 each. This means that he spent $500 in total. Let's suppose that this was a good investment, and a year later, each stock is worth $6.00 apiece. Now Bill has $600 and decides to sell his stocks. He will be taxed for those $600 because those are his 'capital gains.' Properties are not subject to this specific tax, but there are other costs, other than property taxes, that subtract from the capital gains of owning a home.

Insurance, for example can be costly, especially if your tenants abuse of your appliances. The same holds true for other types of maintenance and renovations, which may eat away at your profits. That said, because the capital gains taxes are so high in some parts of the United States, rental properties may be a solid avenue for future investments.

Depending on your perspective, there is another potential 'con' for real estate; it is not as **liquid** as stocks. The liquidity of an asset is essentially how quickly one can buy and sell an asset. In the information age, buying and selling stock is just as easy as clicking some buttons on your computer, rendering stocks more 'liquid' than real estate. In order to buy a home, you need to jump through several legal and financial hoops. The same holds true for selling a home, meaning that real estate is less liquid than the stock market. However, depending on your perspective, real estate is something you can physically touch and feel. To many people, this makes real estate a lot more alive than abstract numbers on your computer indicating whether or not your gains are up on a certain day. Real estate, then, becomes a much more tangible asset that stock market holdings.

Now that we have a basic background on what the pros and cons are for both types of passive investment plans, here are what both stocks and real estate have in common. First, and this is probably the most important commonality, both of these investments are forms of passive income—this means that you don't have to *work* for your money, as you would with any other job. This allows you to actually have a job (if you so wish) while making money on the side. Alternatively, if you invest in enough properties, this becomes your full-time job and you are ready to reap the benefits. There is another subtle point to be made here, which is especially true for our more sensitive readers. When you are investing in real estate, you are providing a service to your tenants. More specifically, you are giving them a roof over their head. The same cannot be said for investing in stocks, where you're often making rich people richer by raising the price of the stocks they already own.

For those who are risk averse, you have to keep in mind that both styles of passive investment—investing in the stock market or real estate—require you to relinquish some of your money. This means that while you may have control over which stocks you buy or which properties you own, the fluctuating prices of these stocks and properties are fundamentally outside of your sphere of influence. That said, as we saw from the figure above, stocks fluctuate much more erratically than real estate.

Where you put your money is a very personal and serious decision that should involve serious thought and planning. Taking into account not only your current living situation, but also your future ones are paramount in ensuring that your investments remain profitable. This may also include the involvement of spouses, children, and family members. Though you may not have children now, if you plan on having kids, selling your home is not as simple as selling stocks. That said, for the purposes of this book, we are assuming that you are interested in learning more about investing in real estate. The next chapter is going to provide you with the basics of real estate investing so you can begin to invest wisely in your future.

CHAPTER 2: THE BASICS OF REAL ESTATE INVESTING

Have you ever played the board game Monopoly? If so, you already have a pretty good background on how real estate investing works. First of all, when you land on a property, say Boardwalk or Park Place, you have the option of buying the lot. If you choose to do so, every time another player lands on your property, they have to pay you 'rent.' The same rules apply no matter where you land on the board, whether its New York Avenue or Ventnor Avenue.[2] If you put $400 to buy Boardwalk, you want every other player in the game to land on your property and have to pay you rent, which for this property is $50 assuming you have not developed it. This means that if you are to make a profit on your investment, other players must land on your property at least eight times to break even.

The professionals call this **return on investment** (ROI). Essentially, this term is the ratio of net profit and cost of the investment. If you dropped $400 for a property, the very least you need to make sure you break even is have other players land on your property eight times (8 x $50 = $400). That return on investment is 1:1, which means that you invested $400 and your returns were also $400. However, if you are to be successful in real

---

[2] For those readers who are into trivia, Monopoly is based off an actual city in the United States. The streets in the original board game are all based off of Atlantic City, New Jersey.

estate investing, your returns must be higher than your initial investments. Your returns must additionally account for taxes, insurance, and utilities. Fail to pay for these taxes and, in Monopoly as in real life, you may end up going to jail (don't pass through Go and don't collect $200).

In Monopoly, there are a few ways to make money. When another player lands on your property, they have to pay you the going rent for the spot. Alternatively, you can sell your property and receive some cash for getting rid of your investment. The same holds true if your property is foreclosed. However, there is only one way to make *real* money in Monopoly. That is if you buy all of the properties of the same color (for example, Pennsylvania Avenue, Pacific Avenue, and North Carolina Avenue are all of the green properties in the classic game). Buying all of the properties of the same color then allows the players to begin constructing houses, and even a hotel on their properties. This extra investment, in turn, forces other players to pay higher rents every time they land on your property. You will find that there are striking similarities between the game Monopoly and real estate investment, not the least of which is how you can make money.

The Two Big Ways To Make Money

Similar to Monopoly, there are two primary ways in which the real estate investor can make money. The first is quite straightforward—**cash flow** income. Cash flow income is a form of passive income stemming from your real estate investments whereby tenants pay you rent. Let's suppose that Kenny in Pennsylvania buys a property on Market Street of his small town and decides to rent out the property to a small family. After scoping out various tenants, Kenny finds a small family that is looking for a place to live. The two parties then agree that they can live in Kenny's property as long as they pay rent every month. This results in cash flow for Kenny, who then can do whatever he likes with the extra money. Unless Kenny has a large amount of capital available however, he likely has to funnel some of those profits from the family's rent to his mortgage for that property. This brings us to the next way an investor can make money[3] from their real estate—appreciation.

Real estate **appreciation** is a long-term way to make money from your investments. Appreciation, also known as capital appreciation, is an economic term showing how the value of an investment can increase over time. The opposite of this phenomenon is **depreciation**. Let's look at some examples. If

---

[3] Technically, there are other avenues for making money off real estate, they just are not what one thinks of as 'real estate.' For example, investing in vending machines in office buildings or laundry machines in large apartment buildings are technically considered real estate, though nobody lives in a vending machine or laundry machine. For the purposes of this book, however, these types of investment strategies will not be discussed, though they may be lucrative for some investors.

Jessica buys a car for $10,000 and uses it for five years, the value of the vehicle is much less than what she originally purchased it for. Perhaps after thousands of miles on the vehicle and technology that is now obsolete, her car isn't worth $10,000 any more. Its worth is likely closer to $2,000.[4] Thankfully, properties do not depreciate in the same way vehicles do. Rather, they tend to appreciate over time. Imagine that at the same time that Jessica bought her car, she also bought a home for $100,000. Ten years later, the technology of the home has not changed much and she cannot really 'use it up' in the same way she can add miles to a car. This means that the value of the home stays relatively the same. So what may cause appreciation?

Appreciation of a home can result from a variety of factors. If Jessica decides to replace the old carpet for hardwood floors, then the value of her property would increase. The same holds true if she replaces the old kitchen cabinets for nice new ones, or if she adds a garage to the property. These actions are all considered **active appreciation strategies**. Essentially, these strategies are additions and renovations to your property that increase its value. They may come in the form of expensive bathroom remodeling

---

[4] Assets can depreciate over time and then begin appreciating again. If Jessica holds on to that vehicle for 60 years, it is now an antique, indicating that its worth may begin to rise again. The opportunity cost, naturally, is that Jessica would not be able to use the car too much and it would take up space in her garage for a generation. Additionally, you can judge for yourself if the return on investment would really be worth it if she needs to hold on to her car for so long.

strategies to changing simple light fixtures that make the property look nicer. Here's the interesting thing about active appreciation strategies – the sum of the parts can be greater than the whole! Small investments to your property can greatly appreciate the value of your investment. If Jessica invests $2000 in simple touches around one of her properties, the total value of the home can increase by *more* than her initial investment, which in this case was $2000.

Here are some simple active appreciation strategies that tend to disproportionately increase the value of your property. First, keep in mind that in the past, bathrooms were only used for their utility. If you have been in an old house from the early 20th century, then you know how small bathrooms used to be. Currently, bathrooms are built to be more luxurious and tend to be much larger. A simple and cheap way to add value to your property is to update the faucets and add granite or marble countertops. The same holds true for the kitchen. Changing light fixtures are another way to active appreciate the value of your hold with little effort and capital. Upgrades in window treatment and curtains can additionally pay dividends in the future. Bringing all of these strategies together can really increase the value of your home by tens of thousands of dollars without you having to invest over a thousand dollars of your capital. Make sure to bring it all together in a common theme, as potential buyers will not like having to replace certain faucets to match others, and so on. Active appreciation strategies can all increase the value of your home, but they can all dent your wallet and take up time. Luckily, there is another way to increase the value of your home—passive appreciation.

Unlike active appreciation where the investor, Jessica in this case, has to dynamically work to increase the value of her property, **passive appreciation** is another tactic that may potentially bring the investor some cash. Passive appreciation refers to those factors that may increase the value of an asset without the owner having to invest any more capital in the property. If Jessica played her cards well, she put her money in a property that is in a good neighborhood with a solid school district. What this ensures is that the value of the home can remain high (or ideally increase) if the neighborhood remains intact. Additional factors, such as development of a nice condo building across the street, increased commercial development in her town by other developers, and more funding for the school district, can all play a role in passively appreciating the value of Jessica's property. The best part? She doesn't have to pay a dime for the appreciation of her property! Her property values increase without any work or capital on Jessica's part. The reader should keep in mind that passive appreciation is essentially a long-term strategy, as neighborhoods do not change too rapidly over time.

There are also some signs that should not go unnoticed when seeking to capitalize upon the passive appreciation of your investments. When buying a property, take a look at the amount of 'green space' around. Interestingly enough, trees increase the property values of many homes and neighborhoods. While you can physically look at the trees around a property for future investment, another very easy way to scope out the area is to go on Google Maps and see how 'green' a neighborhood looks. There is a great amount of information that the future investor can glean from looking at a neighborhood from above. Try it for yourself, and you will likely see that the wealthier neighborhoods are significantly greener than poorer 'gray looking' neighborhoods. That said, trees are not the only way for passive appreciation to work in your favor. Mom and Pop shops, museums, parks, libraries, and coffee shops are other clues that may give the prospective investor a good hint as to which direction the neighborhood is going. In the end, the old saying still rings true today: when it comes to real estate, the most important factors are location, location, location.

How to Begin

Now that we have a decent grasp of how real estate investments can make you money, here is a step-by-step guide to beginning to invest in real estate. For the young reader, probably the best way to begin investing in real estate is by buying a **rental property**. Simply put, a rental property is an investment designed to attract tenants, often called renters, to live in your property. These tenants pay you to stay in your property each month, resulting in a passive income. For young investors and those still in college, the easiest way to do this is by buying a condominium or college-like apartment suite. Condos and dorm-style apartments by and large are the properties requiring the least amount of capital as a **down payment**.

Down payments, also called deposits, are payments used to purchase large assets, usually cars and homes. Here is the beauty of a down payment: you only need to physically possess a fraction of the price of the property for you to put a down payment on a home. The rest of the property can be purchased over time, usually in monthly installments with **interest**. Interest, formerly called usury in the Middle Ages back when it was illegal, has a very technical definition, but in essence, it's the amount that the bank or financial institution charges for lending the borrower capital. Interest is how banks and financial institutions make money off of lending. This all may sound pretty complicated, so below we are going to detail the scenario with a basic example that allows you to understand how the process works.

Thomas is currently a graduate student in Boston and has managed to save up around $30,000 in his bank account over the past few years. Like many young people, he has a few options with what to do with his money. He can save it for a rainy day, keep it under his bed, put it in the bank, invest in the stock market, or buy a rental property. Now Thomas knows that if he saves the money in a bank account, he is effectively losing a fraction of it every year.

Here's the problem with saving money in a bank account—**inflation**. Inflation occurs when there is a increase in the value of goods and services in an economy over time. If suddenly everyone in the United States found themselves with an extra thousand dollars in their bank account, nobody is any richer because prices for goods and services will increase accordingly. For better or worse, money is what some people have and others do not. Thomas knows this very well, meaning that he's left with two primary options for what to do with his $20,000. He can invest in the stock market or in real estate.

As we saw from the previous chapter, there are multiple pros and cons to investing in real estate, but Thomas weighs his chances and decides to take the plunge. Now currently, he is paying rent in university housing, but eventually hopes to move into his own place one day. He finds some nearby apartments in Brookline that seem to be prime real estate properties, and decides to check them out. After doing a bit of research, he finds a condo that has three bedrooms and three bathrooms with a shared living room and kitchen. Since this is part of a larger building, there is no backyard, and the homeowner association governs all of the communal hallways and façade of the building. Here's the problem: this property is currently selling for $120,000. Thomas does not have this kind of capital, but he does have $30,000 saved up in his bank account. However, because he is an astute investor, he knows that he can put a down payment for this Brookline property and then pay the rest off with interest.

The general rule for a down payment is that it's worth 20% of the value of the property.[5] Thomas does some quick math here and determines that the price of the down payment is $24,000 for the $120,000 property. He knows that he has this money, but what will he do with the other $96,000 that he owes for buying the property? For this, Thomas will have to take out a loan from his bank or financial institution. But how will the bank know to trust Thomas with their money? In order to do this they will have to run his credit score.

Credit, stemming from the Latin word for belief or trust, allows a financial institution to provide a borrower (in this case Thomas) with capital without the borrower having to reimburse the institution immediately. This, in turn, incurs **debt** on behalf of the borrower. Debt is essentially the flip side of credit—it's the

---

[5] There are some other types of down payment options that are lower for first-time buyers and those who are cash strapped, but they generally come with a heftier price tag in terms of interest.

money that the borrower owes the creditor. When Thomas asks the bank for a loan, he takes on debit. The bank, in turn, becomes the creditor. The only way for the creditor to make money off these types of transactions is for them to charge Thomas interest, which is the fee for lending him money. But $96,000 is quite a lot of money. How does the bank know that Thomas is trustworthy when he borrows such capital? The answer lies in running a **credit score**.

Remember that 'credit' is Latin for trust. Thomas's credit score then becomes his report card for how trustworthy he is as a borrower. The credit score, also called credit rating, is a numeric number somewhere between the ranges of 250 to 850, depending on the credit bureau conducting the research. By all measures, poor credit rating is any score below 500. Between the ranges of 500 and 600 is average credit, and good credit is above 700. Those with credit ratings in the high 700s and lower 800s are borrowers who are adept at paying off their credit on time. So how does one go about establishing credit? An easy way to get to this first step is by using a credit card. When an individual buys a product with their credit card, they are not charged immediately. Rather, they are effectively taking on debt for one month up until the credit card statement comes in the mail. At the end of the month, they then can pay off their credit card. This builds credit over time (by accruing debt), leading credit card users to establish 'trustworthiness' with money by using their credit cards. If

Thomas pays off his credit card in full and on time every month, then his credit score will continue to increase. The more he buys and pays off, the higher his credit score will be.

If Thomas has had a credit card for five years and makes sure to pay off his bills every month, then his credit score should easily be over 700. The only real way to get your credit score to the low to mid-800s is by incurring a lot of debt, and then *always* paying off your debt in monthly installments.[6] The moment Thomas decides to pay the minimum payment or does not pay his bill on time is the moment his credit score begins to plummet. Let's assume that Thomas is wise with his money, and that he pays his bills on time. A long history of paying your bills on time indicates a good partner for a financial institution's investment, rendering Thomas a viable candidate for the bank's $96,000. Now we must keep in mind here that the bank initially loses money when it loans Thomas the cash for the property. However, as we saw, they'll charge interest on their loans. Thomas then has to choose between

---

[6] The reader should also know this idiosyncrasy about your credit score: the more you look at your credit score, the lower it gets. While *prima facie* this may seem to be highly unfair, you must ask yourself the question credit bureaus are asking about you, namely, "why are you looking at your credit score?" The answer, in reality, is that the only legitimate reason to look at your credit score (other than mere curiosity) is if you want to buy something that is really expensive that you do not have the money for just yet. In order to hedge against these types of dents in your credit score, it is often good practice to check your credit score only once a year, so as to not incur any unnecessary hits on your credit score.

two types of interest that are worth examining in detail, as they both have their pros and cons.

The first type of interest that a bank will loan Thomas is called a **fixed interest loan**. In a fixed interest loan, also called a fixed interest rate, is a loan where the interest rate does not change. In 2018, typical interest rates hover between 4.50 to 6.25%, with lower interest rates being advantageous to the borrower. Generally, if the borrower can put down more than 20% of the down payment, these interest rates can be lowered, as that is a sign of a trustworthy investor. The opposite of a fixed interest loan is a **floating interest loan**, also called a variable interest loan or an adjustable rate. Floating interest loans operate in exactly the opposite direction as fixed interest loans. This is a financial instrument whereby the loan changes over time, depending on many different factors in the economy. In short, over long enough periods of time, those who choose to borrow with floating interest loans tend to pay less in loans than those who incur debt through fixed income loans.

The tradeoff is that, like the stock market, when these interest payments change, so does your loan on the property you bought. With both types of loans, there are two main options: 30-year loans or 15-year loans. Both of these types of loans require interest, but generally those who opt for the 15-year loans tend to incur less interest percentagewise because the principle is paid back in half of the time. However, for that same reason, the mortgage is oftentimes nearly double for the 15-year loan than the 30-year option, because the borrower is paying back the money in half of the time. In the next chapter, we will get to which type of loan—fixed or floating—is better for real estate investing, but let's assume that Thomas opts for the fixed interest loan.

Thomas is now ready to purchase the apartment in Brookline that he has been eyeing for some time. He manages to take out the $96,000 loan from his bank at a 5% interest rate for a 30-year period and drops $24,000 as a down payment. This leaves him with $6,000 in the bank and a new apartment that can hold three people. Since he knows that it makes little sense to buy an apartment, rent it out to others, and then pay rent himself on a separate apartment, Thomas decides to move into his new spot in Brookline. Assuming that the costs of moving furniture and painting the new apartment are negligible, he now has a 30-year mortgage whereby he pays $280 per month plus taxes ($96,000 divided by 360, which is the number of months in 30 years, plus five percent per month).

This may seem like a remarkably low number, but the reader should keep in mind that in addition to the mortgage, Thomas has to pay property and city taxes that go into an escrow account, and a homeowner's association (HOA) fee every month. Most of these charges ultimately get rolled over into his mortgage, which he will pay in a lump sum at the end of the month. While taxes and HOA fees are variable from property to property, let's assume that Thomas has to pay around $800 per month for his apartment.

As an astute real estate investor, Thomas knows that he must rent out the other two rooms to cover his own expenses and turn a profit. We will get to how to pick good tenants in Chapter 4, but for now, let's assume Thomas finds two good roommates—Ryan and Laura. Thomas decides to charge them $900 each for renting out his two extra bedroom, which would net him $1,000 per month ($1,800 in rent from Ryan and Laura, minus the $800 that he pays in his mortgage). Here's where the undisciplined fail: if Thomas is netting $1,000 a month, he has every incentive to pocket the money and spend it on perishable goods and services. He can spend it on a laptop, a fancier car, a nice watch, and so on. However, if he is smart with his money, he will save up those extra $1,000 in a separate account and not touch it. Thomas knows that with $24,000, he was able to buy his first three-bedroom apartment.

The other very important thing to keep in mind is that expenses can eat away at your cashflow. It's extremely important to keep this in mind. Many people spend their cashflow as soon as it comes in, then when something goes wrong in the house (the hot water tank needs replaced, or the basement floods), they will have to come up with the money from somewhere to pay for those repairs and any other type of maintenance on the house. Maintenance, repairs and expenses are inevitable and unavoidable. A smart investor will have a plan in place for these hurdles and will set aside a sizable portion of his cash-flow every month to create a fund to pay for emergencies and maintenance that needs to be handled throughout the life of the mortgage. We will get more in-depth on expenses and how to plan for and manage them in chapter 4.

But back to Thomas and his investment: Here's the tricky part about real estate investing. Buying one property will simply allow you to tread water; buying two properties will help you make a little bit of money; and buying three properties will make you some more, but not help you become rich. If your goal is to get rich off your real estate investments, you must invest in *multiple* properties. If Thomas knows this, then when he collects rent from Ryan and Laura, he'll put them in a separate account, planning to use this in the future. As we saw above, he's doing this, meaning that Thomas would be able to purchase his next three-bedroom apartment at a similar price in two years ($1,000 saved every month for 24 months equates to a 20% down payment on another $120,000 home).

If we fast-forward two years, now we see Thomas with two three-bedroom apartments, with five tenants (he is living in the last apartment). The reader may think that it'll take him another two years after that to purchase the next apartment, but that's not the case. In fact, now Thomas is earning $4,500 from his investments, minus two $800 mortgages for a total of $1,600. This indicates that Thomas is netting $2,900 per month, nearly three times the amount that he was saving two years ago. At this rate, in eight months, Thomas has enough saved up for a *third* apartment. If he is astute enough with his money, he is well positioned to find another similar property within five months after that, and so on *ad infinitum*.

Clearly this is a hypothetical and idealized scenario. It is unlikely that Thomas will find identical apartments over and over again at the exact time he needs them in the same neighborhood. There are also changes in taxes, which may affect his bottom line. Furthermore, it should not be assumed that tenants will stay for extended periods of time, or that they pay their rents as faithfully as Thomas paid his credit card. Also, and many readers may relate to this, life happens. Unless Thomas is an automaton, he may likely dip into his savings account that he created by charging Laura and Ryan rent over the past few years. Furthermore, and many economists still argue about this, buying a property is an *investment*, not a *consumption*.

If Thomas is 'consuming' his home, in the sense that he's messing up the carpets, not taking care of appliances, and damaging the walls, then his equity on his property decreases over time. In this case, his property becomes a consumptive good, rather than an investment. This is an important point to make, as many would-be investors end up 'consuming' their properties rather than keeping its resale value high for the future. Though this situation may be hypothetical, the rest of this chapter is dedicated to helping you stay on track so that you can become a real estate mogul within a short period of time.

The preface to the next section deals primarily with leveraging debt to finance your next projects. Because of this, it is worth explaining here how one can use debt to their advantage. The first step is to understand how **leveraging** works in the real estate market. Leveraging[7] is the use of borrowed capital, such as a property, to increase the potential ROI (the reader will remember that this term means 'return on investment'). Because only 20% of a property needs to be paid for outright, it is in the buyer's best interest to buy the most expensive property possible given the cash on hand. The bank, by leveraging the investments of others using them, buys the other 80% of the property, called the **purchase price**.

Let's look back to Thomas' situation for an example. The reader will recall that Thomas bought a property for $120,000, putting a down payment of $24,000. However, for the sake of argument, let's imagine that Thomas could buy a mobile home for

---

[7] British and Australian readers should note that leveraging is called 'gearing' in your countries. The United States and Canada, on the other hand, use the term 'leveraging.'

$24,000. He would then have no mortgage, and doesn't have to deal with banks, interest rates, and so on. However, if both properties are appreciating at the same value of 4%, then Thomas' property increases by $4,800 per year, meaning that the year after he buys a home, it's now worth $124,800. But what if he bought that $24,000 mobile home? Four percent of $24,000 is $960, meaning that this option is worth $24,960. Notice the price difference? Simply by investing in the more expensive property (leveraging), Thomas accrued a difference of $3,840 in passive appreciation per year, without having to work at all for it. Now imagine multiplying this number after Thomas purchases his fourth and fifth properties.

Now that the reader has a solid background on how leveraging works, it's time to make sure that the property values of investments increase, rather than decrease, because then leveraging has the opposite effect. The next section of this work will discuss how the investor can buy rental properties in different markets, ranging from rural markets to urban markets.

Rural Markets

If you are a future investor, you likely do not want to jump into the deep end of real estate investing by purchasing the most expensive condominium you can afford in downtown Manhattan, just to deal with a punishing mortgage for the next thirty years. It is in scenarios such as these that rural markets play an important role for the future mogul. Rural markets, as one would imagine, tend to be less expensive than downtown centers and urban markets. However, this is not always the case. It really depends in the *type* of rural market.

A hundred years ago, rich people owned properties in urban centers, such as New York and Chicago. The poor, on the other hand, lived in the outskirts of the cities or in rural areas. Currently however, the roles are changing. While many wealthy people still live in urban regions, we are experiencing a change in their patterns, as some very wealthy investors are purchasing rural properties. This is especially true for commercial farms, private ranches, and large estates, which may cost millions of dollars. While at first glance, the reader may be confused as to where to begin with rural markets, here is a neat trick: measure the distance of the rural markets to the nearest city.

Here's an example: let's suppose that Tyler lives in Baltimore and is looking to invest in rural properties near his home. Now for reference, Baltimore is 'happily' ensconced between two large urban areas – Washington, DC to the south, and Philadelphia in the north. Both of these cities, along with Baltimore itself, have their own suburbs, which take up a large portion of the surrounding areas. Therefore, if he is looking for cheaper properties, it is wise to not invest in such places in between Baltimore and Washington, DC. Rather, Tyler should look to the less populated eastern part of Maryland or across the Chesapeake to the west.

Assuming all other factors stay the same (*ceteris paribus* is the technical term in economics), similar properties to the east and west of Baltimore ought to be less expensive than those north or south of Baltimore, because they are closer to other urban areas.[8] That said, every neighborhood is different, so it's always necessary to do your homework in different regions before pouring your money into one property. The general statement does stand: rural properties are cheaper and therefore tend to require less capital to begin investing.

There are a two main advantages and disadvantages to rural properties being less expensive than urban properties. First, as previously hinted, because they are less expensive, the startup cash is not as prohibitive. A major hurdle to first-time investors is collecting the startup cash to purchase your first property. The less expensive rural properties are a major draw for first-timers. On the other hand, in the previous chapter, we saw how investors may leverage their debt to grow their fortunes over time. Well the simple math shows us how cheaper properties do not have much 'leverage' over more expensive ones. Because of this, property owners seeking to turn a profit from rural investments may have

---

[8] If, however, Tyler lives near Sioux Falls, SD, then this situation would play out quite differently. The nearest city to Sioux Falls is Minneapolis, which is 250 miles away. Naturally, in these types of cases, Tyler would not have to worry too much about spillover from nearby urban cities, as they are at a considerable distance from where he's looking to invest.

to be a bit lucky, or invest in *many* properties so that the passive appreciation of property adds to the investor's bottom line.

While there are clearly differences in price between rural and urban properties, there are other nuances that make rural properties a worthwhile investment. First is the difference in **turnovers** between rural and urban properties. The term turnover refers to the number of tenants that come in and out of your properties. Having a single renter in your property for fifteen years is a blessing in the real estate market. Dealing with changes in tenants at a bimonthly basis is painful and you will lose money with empty apartments along with the wear on your properties.

Because rural areas are less populated, there are fewer similar apartments or homes for people to move to, meaning that you are less likely to experience severe turnover in your investments. This stability is great for cash flow purposes, meaning that you will be less likely to be paying the mortgage on empty apartments.

For the same reason that there is little turnover in rural areas, there is also less competition from other investors, meaning that while the pond may be smaller, you're the bigger fish. This is especially true with older rural properties. Not only do they sell for less money, there is also less competition for them. Along this vein, there is an important point to be made. Because rural real estate is less competitive, it is not such a cutthroat industry as urban real estate, which resembles something closer to survival of the fittest. Especially when looking at rural properties, it is important to note that there are huge differences in the types of investments you can make. Barns, farms, and ranches all have different challenges, but one thing holds them all together: they are plentiful in rural areas. This solid supply of properties makes rural communities a viable place for the future mogul to invest their money.

Here's another advantage to rural properties: low taxes. Nothing absolutely destroys your bottom line as having to pay upwards of 60% of your tenants' rents in property taxes. Because rural communities tend to tax less (fewer schools, less infrastructure, etc.), back-end costs to investing in these regions may pay dividends in the long run. After all, taxes are a sunk cost – you cannot recuperate them and your benefits from them are indirect. Aligned with fewer property taxes, rural communities also tend to have less regulation. Since most people in rural communities are spread further apart than they are in urban sectors, it doesn't matter that much what they do in their own homes, leading to less overall regulation. Before we discuss suburban and town real estate markets, it's important to contrast the differences between rural and urban markets. In this spirit, this work will now look at urban markets so the reader can compare the differences with the rural markets.

Urban Markets

The first thing to know about urban markets is that they are all extremely different. Just like in the game Monopoly, the differences between Mediterranean Avenue costing $60 and Boardwalk setting you back $400 are staggering. Unlike rural markets where an investor can clearly notice the differences between an expensive ranch and a run-down barn, these distinctions are blurred in urban markets. On top of this, each city in the United States has a slum and skyscrapers with million-dollar penthouses. The staggering differences between properties in urban markets can leave potential investors lost, so here are some details that may smooth out the transition for the reader.

The first thing the reader should know about urban markets is that prices vary greatly from neighborhood to neighborhood in urban markets. San Francisco and New York are the two most obvious examples of overpriced housing cities in the United States. Take a look at the chart below illustrating the disparity in home values in San Francisco as compared to other cities in California.

Figure 2: Home Prices in California (Source: Winzer 2018)[9]

---

[9] Information taken from https://www.forbes.com/sites/ingowinzer/2018/03/01/investing-in-

California Markets

2018	Population	3-Year Pop. Growth	Job Growth Rate	Home Price Change	Avg. Home Price $(000)	vs Income Price	Price/Rent Ratio
Anaheim	3,114,363	2%	1.0%	6%	623	32%	28
Riverside-San B.	4,380,878	3%	3.3%	9%	300	31%	18
Los Angeles	10,017,068	1%	1.0%	9%	524	23%	28
Oxnard-Ventura	839,620	1%	2.1%	7%	525	16%	24
San Francisco	1,584,815	4%	1.6%	6%	1,097	27%	46
Oakland	2,673,096	4%	1.4%	8%	606	21%	30
Santa Rosa	495,025	2%	0.9%	8%	490	19%	24
San Jose	1,919,641	3%	1.9%	7%	828	18%	32
Vallejo-Fairfield	424,788	4%	1.2%	10%	334	18%	18
San Diego	3,211,252	3%	1.3%	8%	480	18%	24
Sacramento	2,215,770	4%	2.2%	10%	327	15%	21
Santa Cruz	269,419	2%	0.8%	6%	580	23%	29
Santa Maria	435,697	2%	1.9%	6%	487	18%	24
Napa	140,326	1%	2.3%	7%	523	15%	26
San Luis Obispo	276,443	2%	1.2%	6%	471	15%	27
Salinas	428,826	2%	1.1%	8%	441	14%	24
Stockton	704,379	4%	1.1%	10%	282	9%	18
Modesto	525,491	3%	1.9%	9%	244	6%	16
Chico	222,090	2%	1.1%	9%	257	4%	19
Redding	178,980	0%	3.2%	7%	229	2%	16
Fresno	955,272	3%	2.3%	10%	230	-2%	18
Yuba City	168,690	2%	0.5%	13%	304	-2%	26
Hanford	150,960	0%	2.0%	10%	241	-5%	19
Merced	263,228	2%	0.7%	10%	228	-8%	18
Bakersfield	864,124	2%	1.6%	4%	189	-10%	15
El Centro	176,584	2%	1.4%	6%	237	-10%	21
Visalia	454,143	2%	1.3%	8%	208	-15%	18
Madera	152,389	2%	3.6%	9%	258	-19%	18

This chart tells us a lot about the disparity of home prices in one single state. First let's take a look at the notoriously expensive San Francisco. Judging from the average home price column, we see that San Francisco is the only city in California with an average home price of just over a million dollars.

This means that if the investor would like to purchase a property there, they would need substantially more capital ($200,000 for a 20% down payment) than if they were to purchase a property in Bakersfield, with an average property value of

---

california-real-estate-here-are-a-few-things-you-should-know/#3d69d34a6d6e.

$189,000. The down payment for the average home in this city is $37,800, a fraction of the down payment for the average home in San Francisco. Now some readers may be looking at San Francisco with a jaundiced eye, so here is some more information on expensive urban markets that may sway your mind.

First, the reader must always keep in mind that there is a reason why San Francisco is expensive. It's an ideal place to live. The weather is great year round, tenants are close to both the ocean and mountains, high-tech jobs are plentiful and nearby, and the city has a vibrant culture that attracts Millennials and **empty nesters** [10] alike. Due to the combination of these factors, San Francisco enjoys not only high property values, but also *better* properties. This ultimately would increase the average price of properties in the city, hence the million-dollar row homes and brownstones. As is often stated in real estate, location is the best predictor of success.

Next, not all of us have $200,000 lying around to invest in one property. This leads us to point out the second nuance when looking at the San Francisco market: you don't have to buy the most expensive property, or even the average-priced property. Just because the average price of a home in San Francisco is over a

---

[10] The term 'empty nesters' often refers to those parents whose children have grown up and left home, leaving their original property comparably empty.

million dollars doesn't mean that there aren't cheaper alternatives.

When analyzing real estate markets in expensive cities, such as Los Angeles or New York, make sure to determine price differences between various neighborhoods. This is another advantage urban markets have over rural ones. The investor can differentiate between property prices in the same neighborhood. This type of homogeneity is unlikely to be found in rural communities, where similar cookie cutter properties do not exist. Along this vein, it is also a good idea to scrutinize how these properties have changed in price over time. The next chapter includes some useful tips and tricks for the first-time investor on this issue.

Let's take a second look at the urban markets in California. Naturally, we see San Francisco, Anaheim, Oakland, and Los Angeles as enjoying (or suffering from) expensive housing markets, but what about the changes in price of these markets? Every city in California is experiencing an increasing in housing value over time, as we don't see any negative numbers in the 'Home Price Change' column above. However, some markets are increasing at a faster rate than others. It sure looks like San Francisco is plateauing at a 6% increase in home values, though this is still pretty good. Yet, take a look at Fresno, Yuba City, Merced, Hanford, Sacramento, and Stockton. All of these cities are experiencing growth at double-digit rates, with Yuba City reaching a 13% change in home price. For the real estate investor thinking of investing in urban markets, these properties offer the highest

ROI in terms of passive appreciation. But how does the future investor know what to expect in terms of rent for their urban properties?

As the reader will recall from the previous section, there are two primary ways to make money in the real estate market: rent from tenants and property appreciation. If the investor is looking for property appreciation, they will do well to look at the red column in *Figure 2* denoting 'Home Price Changes.' Yet, how can the investor know what to charge for rent? Simple, use the 1% rent rule. This rule states that the average value a property can be rented out for is 1% of the total cost of the property.

So, let's imagine that Matt holds a property in Modesto, CA that costs around $250,000, which is about average for that city. Since Matt is a profit-maximizer, he is looking to rent out his property for the most amount of money. However, if the price is too high, then nobody will rent out Matt's property and he will have to lower his price. This creates a balance—a sweet spot of sorts—between the prices that a renter is willing to pay versus the price an investor wishes to charge. If Matt is familiar with the 1% rent rule, then he can find this balance quite easily. He simply takes 1% of $250,000, which is $2,500 and charges that figure for rent. If Matt's property is a condo with multiple bedrooms and bathrooms, then he has the opportunity to split that rent between two or three tenants.

There is another advantage to investing in urban properties over rural ones. Urban properties are remarkably easy to resell. Because of the lower level competition in rural markets, there are fewer people vying for fewer properties, rendering such markets more difficult if the investor is looking for a **fixer-upper** or to turn properties quickly. Fixer-uppers, as the name suggests, are those often-foreclosed properties that an investor buys at a discount from a bank, fixes them up, and then resells them for a profit.

This style of real estate investing works much better in urban markets that in rural markets precisely because of the fast resale rates of urban markets. Put in economic terms, urban markets are more 'liquid,' meaning that they can be turned into cash on hand, than rural markets. This work will touch upon the benefits and drawbacks of using different types of loans (e.g., hard money loan) for fixer-uppers in the later chapters. But for now, it's important for the future mogul to know that this is a way to invest in the urban real estate market, if done correctly, for some serious profits.

Yet another advantage to the urban market is property appreciation. As hinted by the figure in the previous pages, urban markets in California are all appreciating in value, yet at different paces. Some, like San Francisco, seem to be plateauing while others, such as Fresno, are booming. As a general rule of thumb, the investor should be wary of small percentages of appreciation in value in smaller cities. Investing in a shrinking economy is generally not a good idea, especially if this economy correlates with a shrinking population. Rural markets move on a much slower time scale, thereby appreciating at far gentler a rate than urban markets.

Suburban Markets

When investors talk about different real estate markets, they tend to simply differentiate between rural and urban regions, assuming that suburbs are simply the halfway point to both markets. This could not be further from the truth. Suburbs may as well be their own animal when it comes to real estate investing, so this section is dedicated to showing you how to differentiate between suburban properties and where the pros and cons are for this market. First and foremost, as an investor, the last situation you want is empty rooms with a mortgage. These scenarios force the investor to continue paying for the home, along with taxes and insurance, without tenants actually using the homes themselves and paying rent.

With this knowledge in mind, a unique and positive characteristic of the suburban real estate market is the slow turnover rate. The reader will recall that turnover is the changing of tenants over and over again. As an investor, this unreliability in renters creates more paperwork, leaves more to chance, leaves apartments empty, and leads to less stability.

All of these factors increase uncertainty and lead to less confidence in investing. Luckily, suburban markets are reliably stable. Tenants choosing to live in suburban markets tend to have small families, have stable jobs, can pay rent, and tend to save money. Because of this, they often prefer more permanent locations. When investing in suburban real estate markets, pay special attention to the school districts there, as many parents with young children will move to better school districts so that their children can have a better education than they would have elsewhere. If your property can attract these tenants, you will likely have renters in these properties for a long time.

The downside to these more permanent tenants is that there may be a lack of interest in renting. Most people who live in suburbs are small families or those looking to have a family of their own in the future. This means that there may be an overall interest buying homes rather than renting them for long periods of time. However, as previously stated, if they have small kids, they may interested in changing homes due to more competitive school districts in some neighborhoods over others. Where the future investor can distinguish herself is in knowing their clients and their needs. The real issue here is that those who live in suburbs are accustomed to 'owning' their possessions. They likely have their cars paid off, have their own furniture, and are generally more interested in owning a home as well. Connected to owning a vehicle, there is additionally a general lack of public transportation in suburban parts of the United States. While it is nearly impossible to move in urban areas without public transportation, very few buses and subways reach suburban communities.

Connected to the permanence of the tenants in suburban markets is that they tend to treat your properties with greater care. Because of this, the appliances of the home tend to be taken care of at a better rate than in urban sectors where tenants may move from property to property with little care for the appliances. Since many children are living in these suburban properties, parents usually wish to teach them good cleaning and maintenance habits, leading these units to be a better 'bang for your buck' as an investor. This respect for your property goes a long way in its resale value, especially if your tenants view your property as a home, rather than as a temporary living space.

Another unique characteristic of suburban real estate is the sheer difference in size per square foot of property. Let's suppose that Sean is looking to either invest in Tulsa city proper, or one of its surrounding suburbs. If he is looking for a $200,000 property, he can likely get a unit with 2000 square feet in Tulsa, or 6000 square feet of property in one of its suburbs. This three-fold increase in suburban property sizes makes the investor 'feel' as if they have more property, and ultimately equates to more physical property than investing in urban sectors. Combined with this extra space is a backyard. Many tenants hoping to have a quieter life in the suburbs enjoy properties with some space. It then follows logically that if you are thinking of investing in the suburbs, the properties you look for should have at least a small backyard or a large-enough front yard.

There are two more, intertwined, aspects of investing in suburban properties. First, suburbs have a huge decrease in crime rate as compared to urban centers. This naturally renders them more appealing to families looking for safety for their children. Along this track, suburbs tend to also be quieter than urban areas, though, of course, not as quiet as rural properties. Many suburbs also offer enough evening activities to keep adults busy without overloading them with the constant neon glow of city lights. Suburbs are usually home to high school football stadiums, guilds, societal clubs, and the like that provide enough entertainment for tenants without forcing them into overdrive. Suburbs are also much more spread out than urban areas, but since many homes are similar, purchasing various single-property homes in one suburb is a viable investment option for the future real estate investor.

The final characteristic of suburbs is the location. They are far away enough from cities that these properties are not as loud, but not in rural parts of the United States that lack amenities. Suburbs offer easy-enough access to city life should tenants choose to go into the city, while offering the accommodations of more space and tranquility in rural regions. As with any suburb, there are dozens of different neighborhoods that offer a variety of income levels and properties for investment. Real estate investment strategies may change from neighborhood to neighborhood, contingent upon school districts, crime, and noise levels by restaurants and bars.

Now that the reader has a decent idea of how to make money as a real estate investor and knows how to differentiate between urban, rural, and suburban markets, it is now time to discuss the differences between tenants. There are two primary types of investments: single-family real estate investment and multi-family real estate investment. Let's take a look below at the two different types of investments and how they differ.

Single-Family Real Estate Investing

Single-family real estate investing, as the name suggests, denotes a type of home fit for a single family. These homes tend to be smaller and quainter than multi-family homes. Almost every example in this book thus far suggests that the reader is interested in single-family real estate investing. Here are a few tips and tricks to ensuring that your single-family real estate investing goes off to a successful start. The first suggestion is to not get emotional about the properties you are buying. These are investments we are talking about. It doesn't matter if you prefer one color of home to another or if the tiles in the home were similar to those in the house you grew up in.

These emotional factors can really skew the future investor's perspective when buying a home. Remember that your investment depends upon movement in the market and not independent feelings about your childhood. Along this train of thought, here's a common mistake that many investors make: they think that if something existed or went wrong with their homes as children, they have to account for (or live with) those changes as an adult.

Here's an example. Let's imagine that Jackson in Alabama grew up in a lower middle-class home. Drains were always clogged and the heater often didn't work in the winter. After Jackson grew up, he wanted to invest in real estate to escape his lower-middle class living in the American South. He decides to invest in some single-family homes and rent out the rooms to tenants for profit. However, his tenants keep telling him that the heater is inconsistent and unreliable. Jackson may think to himself, "this is not such a bad problem. After all, I had to pass multiple winters in the cold when I was a child and I still survived." This type of thinking may lead to a quick turnover of tenants as Jackson isn't taking care of a necessity of his tenants in a timely manner. Though something may have been a problem when the investor was a child, this may not be a good practice to continue with future tenants. Amazingly enough, the opposite also occurs. We will explain below.

Geoff is coming from an up and coming family living near Seattle. He wants to continue his family trajectory of being a successful businessman, so he begins investing in real estate for single-family homes. Because he comes from a relatively privileged background, he hopes to purchase and remodel homes at relatively high prices to retain tenants. Because of this, he *over* furnishes his properties. But what does this mean?

By making too many improvements to a home, Geoff accomplishes two things. First, he invests a lot of extra capital in his properties because hardwood floors, updated kitchens and cabinets, and built-in bookcases can be quite expensive. Second, the upgrades are meant to be used by tenants, meaning that their resale value shouldn't be taken into account yet. Significant wear and tear will occur by tenants before the property is up for sale. This wear and tear drastically depreciates the value of the property before it is resold, meaning that a lot of Geoff's investments—though they may be well intentioned—may end up losing him money.

What makes single-family real estate investing so easy and lucrative is that there are few barriers to entry. The investor realistically only needs to possess 20% of a property as a down payment to launch a career in real estate investing. As we all know, this is much easier said than done. A common mistake made by young investors is to think they are purchasing investments. This is incorrect thinking. What investors are doing is closer to starting a business than accruing properties.

Therefore, their properties should be considered business investments rather than a place to put their money. As a special, but necessary side note, it is *always* in the young investor's best interest to not seek friends or family as tenants. Family and friends, though they may be blessings in real life, make for poor tenants. Because they are much more familiar with you and know how many properties you own, they may feel more comfortable with paying rent late, or not at all. This may lead to not only a loss in revenue, but also unnecessary tension between your friends and your business.

Single-family real estate investing has many potential benefits, but when we compare them to multi-family real estate investing, there are some significant drawbacks. The next section of this book will compare and contrast the differences between single- and multi-family real estate investing. Ultimately, you have to determine which option is best for you, but as with anything in life, starting off is usually the hardest part. In the next section, the reader will realize how this is the case with multi-family real estate investing, and also note how larger up-front investments may pay off in the long run.

Multi-Family Real Estate Investing

As the name suggests, **multi-family real estate investing**, also called apartment complex real estate investing, are properties and buildings with more than one rental space. As hinted in the previous section, these properties require a lot more start-up capital, often called **overhead costs**. The overhead costs for multi-family properties are higher because these units must be bought in bulk. Apartment buildings are only cost efficient if many apartments are side by side. If apartments were far away from each other, the developer would lose significant comparative advantage.

While multi-family real estate investing requires more start-up cash, it is much easier to finance. Don't take my word for it though; here is what real estate investor Warren Cassell states on multi-family complexes: at first sight, "it might seem as though securing a loan for a single-family property would be a lot easier than trying to raise money for a million dollar complex but the truth is a multi-family property is more likely to be approved by a bank for a loan than the average home" (Cassell 2018). The reason that banks are more likely to approve of a loan for apartment complexes and multi-family homes is that they know that apartments generate a lot of cash flow for investors.

This is where **economies of scale** come into play. While this sounds like a complicated term, economies of scale are the cost advantages that investments receive due to their scale, whereby the cost of each additional unit of investment decreases with every increase in the number of units. I know this sounds complicated, but here's an example. Let's suppose that your aunt, Jemima, is baking cookies for her new business. She has an oven that can bake two-dozen cookies at a time, and it takes her an hour to bake all of the cookies. If she wants to bake a single cookie, it takes her two minutes of prep time and then one hour of baking, for a total of 62 minutes. However, if she wants to bake two-dozen cookies, then she takes 48 minutes of prep time plus another hour of baking for a total of 108 minutes.

Let's do the math here: for one cookie, Jemima must spend 62 minutes of her time, but for 24 cookies, she spends 108. Clearly, it is worth her while to bake two-dozen cookies at a time and sell them for profit, rather than baking one cookie at a time. This is the power of economies of scale. Because her oven can bake one cookie or 24 cookies within the same time period, it behooves Jemima to bake 24 cookies at a time. The same rules apply for multi-family real estate investing.

Here's an example of Becky who owns a few single-family properties in a suburban neighborhood. If a tenant vacates a property, Becky is left paying 100% of the mortgage. This is a steep position to be in. However, let's suppose that Warren owns an apartment complex that houses twenty families. If one of his tenants vacates their property, Warren still has 95% of his tenants paying rent, meaning that he can absorb the costs of a unit being empty for a time. In times such as these, banks understand that foreclosures for apartment complexes tend to be rare. For this reason, they are much more likely to give out loans to those seeking to invest in apartment complexes over single-family homes. These are the benefits that economies of scale can provide for those investors who put their money in multi-family apartment complexes.

The next advantage multi-family real estate investments have is geographic homogeneity. As we previously saw, all of the tenants in an apartment complex live in a single building, or sometimes a small set of buildings. This is in stark contrast to single-family real estate investing, where tenants may be spread out across various neighborhoods and cities. If the investor wishes to visit the property for whatever reason, they can check out twenty or thirty homes at once instead of having to drive to multiple sites. By the same token, if repairs, installations, and upgrades need to be made, the investor can more easily hire a handyman or electrician to make all of the changes across twenty units in only one site.

Over time, this geographic homogeneity saves time, effort, and money for future investors. Additionally, repairs for apartment buildings tend to be the same for every unit, indicating that you may only need to hire one contractor and have them do the work twenty times over in the same style of unit. This again is in sharp contrast to single-family properties where each home and apartment has unique designs, rooms, and appliances.

Yet another advantage to multi-family real estate investing is the savings in back-end costs for down payments and loans. Let's assume that David buys fifteen single-family homes in Miami. He would have to draw up fifteen different loans, put fifteen different down payments for each property, and pay fifteen home inspectors for their assistance. Additionally, he would have to account for fees and taxes relating to each of the properties he owns. All of these factors combined can lead to thousands of dollars spent not on his properties, but in back-end costs. Now let's see what Christina is doing in Pennsylvania. She bought one apartment complex that houses fifteen families. With this option, only one loan is necessary to strike the deal with the bank. Additionally, she only needs to draw up one contract, seek the assistance of only one home inspector, and so on. The economies of scale are clearly working in her favor!

The last aspect of multi-family real estate investing relates to property management. Because this is a rather large topic, we will dedicate a small section to the pros and cons of using a property management company below.

Property Management Companies

There are a few advantages to using a property management company, but first a definition is in order. A **property management company** is an entity that manages the investments, or properties, of an investor for them. Now it's important to note that not all property management companies are created equally. Property management companies are supposed to do the hands-on work that the investor delegates to them, so here are a few pointers to determine how good a property management company is for your business.

First, one should get recommendations from colleagues and tenants to determine how a property management company operates its business. If you find yourself in a place without reliable data regarding property management companies, here are two websites that can help you refine your search. The first is the Institute of Real Estate Management (IREM), found at www.irem.org. When you click on their website, make sure to check out the 'Find a Professional' section for ratings of property management companies. The next useful website is the National Association of Residential Property Managers' (NARPM) website, found at www.narpm.org. Once you are on the main page, click to search for property managers. There exist smaller websites for property management companies, but these are the two largest ones.

So, what does a property management company do? According to Leshnower, property management companies "deal directly with prospects and tenants, saving you time and worry over marketing your rentals, collecting rent, handling maintenance and repair issues, responding to tenant complaints, and even pursuing evictions" (Leshnower 2018).[11] Especially if you are new to property management companies, they give the investor the opportunity to bring know-how and experience to your properties, which may help you sleep better at night. Property

---

[11] Information taken from https://www.nolo.com/legal-encyclopedia/landlord-hire-property-management-company-29885.html.

management companies also insulate you as an investor. If tenants have complaints or if something is going wrong with their apartment, they go to the property management company, and not the investor, rendering this alternative a more hands-off approach to real estate investing.

This begs the question: when should the investor hire a property management company? Let's suppose that Rick holds various single-family real estate investments in the suburbs of Houston. All of his properties are spread across five or six neighborhoods and each home is widely different from the next. If this is the real estate strategy that Rick picked out for himself, a property management company makes very little sense. They would lose geographic closeness, property construction homogeneity, and similar tenants.

Now let's suppose that Jesse holds an apartment complex in the outskirts of Houston. All of his units are in one building, their construction is identical from unit to unit, and he charges the same amount for all tenants, rendering all from more or less the same economic spectrum. It would be in Jesse's best interest to use a property management company, because of the same economies of scale described above. The more rental units an investor has, and the more similar the units are, the more the investor gains from using a property management company. Additionally, on the other side of the coin, property management companies would be hesitant to take on Rick's style of real estate investing, as they would spend too much time going from property to property, and lose the homogeneity found in apartment complexes. In short, the time to subcontract out a property management company is when the investor owns multi-family real estate, and not when they own a variety of single-family homes.

Property management companies are particularly useful when the investor does not live near the apartment complexes he or she owns. Being able to drive to your investments is a way to keep a hands-on approach to your investing, but if the apartment complex is a hundred miles away, the investor is better off hiring a property management company. These entities also give the investor a lot of free time to pursue other goals. If the investor finds that tenants are suddenly inundating them with problems and issues, it may be worth their while to invest in a property management company. This is especially true if the investor does not want the hands-on approach that comes with investing in single-family rental units.

Many readers may have probably already spotted the problem with property management companies. They cost money. You now need to hire staff to take care of the work you do not want to do. Holding a property management company is a viable option only if the investor can afford the costs and outsource the work to another group. When approaching property management companies, it is important to note that their quotes usually range between 6% and 10% of the revenue the investor collects in rent. If the reader finds a property management company asking for more than 10%, they should begin interviewing other prospects. The same can be said if a property management company swears that they can do the work for only 3% or 4% of the rental price. Sometimes it is better to pay more for good service than less for bad service.

A poor property management company will repel tenants, lead to dissatisfaction with renters, and ultimately contribute to a higher turnover rate. However, a good property management company works *with* the investor to not only keep tenants, but to also solve their individual problems and address their concerns.

CHAPTER 3: IN-DEPTH STRATEGIES FOR RENTAL REAL ESTATE INVESTING

The reader now has a general idea of best practices for real estate investing. This chapter is designed to advance your understanding of the business strategy, along with including some tips and tricks to make sure you don't fall into bad habits. The bulk of this chapter will include these tips and tricks. Yet, before we begin with that section, it is incumbent upon me as the author to illustrate how a long-term strategy benefits the future investor.

Remember the chart showing the price changes of homes over time since the 1980s? How about the Monopoly game analogy? What both of these topics have in common is that the investor (player in Monopoly) is forced to take a long-term view when investing in properties. Nobody makes a million dollars overnight investing in real estate, and nobody wins a Monopoly game in a half hour. Both of these situations bend toward long-term investments. There are two major strategies to setting long-term goals and raking in the money as a real estate investor. The first option likely applies to the reader, which is investing with little capital.

If you are like most people, you likely do not have one hundred thousand dollars stashed away to invest as a down payment for an apartment complex. This means that you have to resort to single-family real estate investments for the time. Most people can afford to save twenty or thirty thousand dollars throughout their 20s, though this may be a difficult task. Developing a long-term strategy for this money is paramount throughout this time. If the reader invests their money wisely, they can afford to live the life Thomas in Chapter 2 made for himself within ten years or less. As the reader knows, the initial down payment for the first property is the greatest hurdle to overcome when investing in real estate. However, once this hurdle is initially overcome, the real estate investment game is largely a matter of discipline.

Developing a long-term strategy changes from situation to situation, but the pattern described below is a solid strategy for those looking to become real estate moguls. Here's the bottom line: every penny collected in rent from your first tenant must be saved for your future investment! Stash it away in a separate bank account, put it in a CD, or hide it under your bed. Whatever you do, do not touch it. This is the future of your investment strategy and the most important money you will be bringing into your business. The reader should never expect to live off of someone else's rent. This means that for the first two years or so, they will likely have full-time jobs and living off that money, and not the cash coming in from their first investment.

As the reader will remember, the 1% rent rule more or less determines the renting price of a unit compared to the price of the property. This means that the return on investment (ROI) is 100 months, or 8.3 years.[12] However, in order to put the cash down for the next property, the investor must have only 20% of the price for a down payment, meaning that in an ideal world, this can be done in as little as two years. By then, the investor would have two

---

[12] In addition to this 100-month period, the investor can always choose to sell the property, meaning that the ROI of a property is actually much greater than the sum of the rents it has accrued over time from tenants.

properties with potentially two or three people paying rent. This leads to a half-life strategy of real estate investing.

While the term half-life comes from chemistry denoting the time required for a quantity to reduce to half its initial value, this logic applies to real estate investing. *Ceteris paribus*, if it took an investor two years to reach 20% of a property's value in rent from a tenant, it should take *half* that time with two properties, a quarter said time with three properties, an eighth of time with four properties, a sixteenth of time with five properties, and so on.

Notice the pattern here: the number of properties increases in a linear fashion (e.g., 1, 2, 3, 4, and 5 properties), yet the time it takes to turn a profit on these investments decreases exponentially, not linearly (e.g., 2 years, 1 year, 6 months, 3 months, and 1.5 months). This is the half-life logic of real estate investing—it works most efficiently when the investor keeps buying properties. Staying at one or two single-family units does not do the trick. You have to continue buying properties and reinvesting those profits in the next property.

Remember, for the first few years, you will not be able to live off of these properties and you should not touch rents collected from them. You need to reinvest that money in your next property. Once the half-life cycle becomes too time consuming is when you can begin phasing out your full-time job for managing properties. Eventually, if the investor does not want to spend so much time dealing with tenants and can pay for it, they can hire a property management company. One property will keep you from being lower class; two or three will keep you middle-class; but if you want to be rich, you need to own over eight properties, collect rent from all of them and then continue reinvesting those rents for your ninth and tenth properties. While in your 20s and 30s, you won't have the nicest cars or the flashiest jewelry, but you'll be much wealthier for the rest of your life.

Unlike chemistry, where half-lives are predictable, in real estate investing, discipline is king. Many moguls fail to reach these heights because of lack of discipline; they always tap into the rent collected from their first tenants, and don't manage to increase their savings. Even if the reader does not have much initial capital, within four years, they may be able to invest in five properties and collect rent from all of them. That's how simple the process is; *simple*, not easy. Naturally, this is an idealized version of history as tenants may move, properties may not all be the same price, and appliance repairs may be costly. However, as a general rule of thumb, this is the long-term strategy that works most often when jumping into the real estate market.

The second long-term strategy to become a real estate mogul is if the reader already possesses $100,000 in capital. If this is the case, then the solution is easy: do *not* invest in single-family properties. It is much more of a headache than it's worth if you have such capital. The most efficient use of such money in the real estate market is through buying apartment complexes and other multi-family properties. The economies of scale are already in your favor if you already have such capital, meaning that your long-term strategy should look into capitalizing upon the geographic homogeneity, similarity of tenants, and stable profit returns characteristic of multi-family investments.

The reader will quickly notice the difference between the first strategy and the second. The second strategy likely takes a year or two to realize, but the first strategy takes much longer. Welcome to capitalism: this is the world of have-nots and have-yachts.[13] Be careful to not find yourself on the wrong side of that line. That said, after the first few years of reinvesting savings from single-family properties, there is nothing stopping the investor from taking the plunge and buying their first apartment complex. It's simply a tougher road. As a first-time investor, you will make mistakes, but here are some tips and tricks with the most common mistakes and how to avoid them.

Tips and Tricks For Real Estate Investing

If you are looking to successfully invest in real estate, there is some basic knowledge that you should have before you commit money to such an endeavor. This section of the book will help you

---

[13] This term was originally coined by Niall Ferguson in *The Ascent of Money*.

'stand on the shoulders of giants' so to speak. Instead of making the same mistakes many other people have made in the past, it is best to check out their mistakes and seek to avoid repeating them. It is in this spirit that this section offers ten tips and tricks for real estate investing.

Tip 1: Specialize

The first tip is to specialize your real estate investments into one type of property. We're assuming that you have a finite number of resources and limited money. However, the real estate industry is nearly limitless: there are millions of different homes to choose from, along with thousands of different types of properties, ranging from split-levels to mansions. So how do you choose which type of rental property to invest in if you are looking into real estate? After all, there are vacation properties, time-shares, single family homes, multi family homes, townhomes, commercial properties, industrial properties, agriculturally focused properties, and even warehouse rentals (although not particularly romantic, warehouses are surprisingly lucrative). Again, the first tip is to be specific in the rental property that you choose. All of these types of properties have specific codes, taxes, and surcharges, and if you do not specialize in a particular type of property, you may end up losing money. It therefore behooves you to narrow down your decisions and pick a single *type* of property to begin your real estate investing.

We must keep in mind that specialization is key to succeeding in the modern world, but there are some inherent risks in specializing in one type of property that are worth mentioning. Let's suppose that Siobhan in Dublin is seeking to invest in vacation spots in the west coast of Ireland. She scopes out some quaint cottages by the coast and buys some vacation properties, hoping that holiday goers will stay in her little cottages while on vacation. What would happen if Ireland experiences an economic downturn and people stop going on vacation? Well, Siobhan would have to continue paying her mortgages for her rental properties, but they would be empty.

What if she tries selling them? This is another option, but if Ireland experienced this economic downturn after Siobhan bought her vacation homes, then she would be selling them at a lower rate than the price when she bought the cottages. In real estate investing, this reality is something that must always be in the back of our minds; however, many of us think the risks and subsequent benefits are worth the potential costs.

Tip 2: Develop a Plan

If you have already read this far into this book, then you are halfway to making this tip work for you. Investing your life savings in real estate makes little sense if you do not have a plan to back it up. This includes determining how much capital up front you are willing to part with to make your first investment. This author suggests creating that number in your head before you begin searching for properties. This will allow you to set reasonable expectations before you set to work.

Another facet of developing a sound plan is to study how rental properties work. Keep in mind that because there are so many different types of rental properties, each type will react differently to market stimuli. For example, an economic downturn may lead people to losing their homes, thereby increasing the percentage of people *renting* properties. However, the same economic downturn that caused individuals and families to begin renting means that the value of vacation properties and time-shares will accordingly drop. Even though the same economic downturn occurred, different types of properties react differently in the market.

When determining what your plan is for your real estate investments, keep in mind the hidden costs of settling to buy a property. It is often the case that real estate agents, lawyers, condominium associations, and previous homeowners may seek to get their share of the action. Real estate investing, especially as a beginner, is usually a solitary endeavor until you get your fee wet. Along this vein, there are hidden costs to conducting business. School taxes, property taxes, second home taxes, management fees, homeowners association fees, closing fees, and so on can erode any gains you made in your initial buys. Furthermore, these taxes and fees are all different in each US state and city, meaning that you need to get familiarized with the local codes and taxes before investing in a new property. I assume that you do not like surprises, and the fewer there are when it comes to taxes and fees, the happier you will become.

Tip 3: Build a Community

If you are reading this in the United States, there is a good chance that there is a real estate convention occurring sometime in the near future in a convention space near you. These conventions are a great space for networking, exchanging ideas, meeting investors, and even finding prime properties at a discount. These conventions are also a good way to pick investors' brains on which books to read, which states and cities to avoid, how to manage homeowner association fees, and so on. While not a lot of work gets done in these conventions, the rewards from active networking more than pays for the cost of the event. However, conventions are not the only way to build your real estate community.

In order to successfully invest in real estate, you will be better off getting to know other real estate agents, homeowners, and property managers. They have unique and specialized information about the market you may be trying to penetrate. The worst thing for a landlord is to have to act like a loan shark in getting your rental money. Knowing the right people and building your community can hedge against such risks.

Tip 4: Do not Invest in Your Own Name

For risk management issues, it is almost always in your best interest to not buy properties in your own name. There are plenty of other options that will help you both avoid risks and still allow you to buy properties. A viable option for consideration is holding properties through special types of legal entities. This means that, if you live in the United States, you can use a **limited liability company** (LLC). Other countries may have their own specific terms for this type of company. Limited liability companies, as the name suggests, are companies that absorb liability costs from investments while leaving the entrepreneur or CEO's personal finances out of its jurisdiction. This means that if an LLC goes bankrupt, you yourself do not have to also go bankrupt, hence the 'liability' part of the company. The 'limited' part of the LLC refers to any extra-jurisdictional activity. For example, if you do not pay your taxes, not only does your company go bankrupt, you can also lose your personal property because you broke the law. It is usually wise to set up an LLC for your real estate investments to hedge against extraneous factors that will simultaneously help you sleep at night, provided you pay your taxes and don't defraud tenants.

Another option is to set up a limited partnership (LP) or a **limited liability partnership** (LLP). In a limited liabilities partnership, you can share liabilities among other partners in your company, rendering it a safer alternative than LLCs. However, if you decide to go this route, there are a few things to keep in mind. First, you need partners you can trust. Second, make sure to set the parameters of liability and profits before you begin investing and resist changes to such parameters unless something drastic happens in your LLP. Finally, make sure to hire a qualified attorney to go over the details of your contracts with your partners and tenants. Attorneys will also be able to inform you of which type of ownership method, LLC or LLP, is best suited for your needs.

Both of these options are also good if something happens to one of your properties and a renter decides to sue you. Though such cases are legitimate headaches and should be generally avoided (legal fees, courtroom costs, attorneys, and headaches associated with this are usually not worth the settlements), if you have an LLC or LLP set up, you can protect your personal assets though your company may lose money. Should you like more information about how to set up LLCs and LLPs, the US Small Business Administration (https://www.sba.gov) offers a whole host of details on the process and paperwork for these two types of ownership methods.

Tip 5: Go for Fixed Interest Loan

In the last chapter, we discussed the differences between fixed and floating interest loans. While over time a borrower would be able to save money investing with a floating interest loan, this becomes a dangerous practice when you multiply this effect across dozens of properties. If you are investing in multiple properties and all of your interest loans are flexible, then they potentially can all increase or decrease *at the same time*! Not only does this indicate that the borrower would be paying more for a set period of time, this creates a backend headache in accounting. How does one keep the books in order with floating interest rates across a dozen properties? Save yourself the nightmare (along with the emotional baggage that comes with it) and go for the fixed interest loan. It is true that with a fixed interest loan you will likely pay more over time, but what you save in headaches is worth the stability in your investments.

Tip 6: Avoid Flood Plains

To some, this may seem like an obvious tip, but there are a surprising number of homes being built on flood plains. Don't believe me? Turn on any news station in the summer, and you'll see dozens of homes destroyed due to hurricanes and torrential storms pouring down water in some regions of the United States. Unlike earthquake-resistant homes and wind-resistant windows, flooding utterly destroys the resale value of a property. When the home inspection is done to ensure that the property you are buying has nothing wrong with it, make sure to look at whether or not it's in a flood plain. Any experienced home inspector will be able to easily inform the buyer of the risk of flooding.

To be sure, there are several ways to hedge against flooding damage. The best example is buying flood insurance. Here's the tricky and painful truth about purchasing flood insurance: only properties in flood plains need insurance, which, in turn, are those exact properties that tend to be flooded. Because of this, flood insurance in non-flood plains tends to be relatively inexpensive, as insurance companies are not betting that these properties will flood. The opposite, however, is also true. Properties in flood plains tend to have extraordinarily high insurance rates *because* they get flooded more often.

There's another downside to flooding – it is not localized. What this means is that if there is flooding in one property, say near a river, there likely will be flooding in other nearby properties. When one company insures all of the properties along the river that are in the flood plain, they may find themselves having to pay out to each property owner more money than they have on hand. This may bankrupt the company, thereby leaving all those insured with no recovery costs *despite* their monthly payments to the insurance company. By law, insurance companies must keep a certain amount of cash on hand to hedge against such scenarios, but if you are looking to invest in real estate, this risk is likely not worth taking.

Tip 7: Track Price Changes in a Property Over Time

Before you put a down payment on a property, it is incumbent upon you to track the price of the property throughout time. This will give you a good idea of the direction the property is heading. Unlike the stock market that has erratic changes in value on a day-to-day basis, the real estate market investor knows that changes come slowly and over long periods of time. Because of this, we can quite accurately track the price changes of properties over time by looking at their history. When you analyze price differences, make an Excel spreadsheet to compare the price of the property you are eyeing to the prices of nearby similar lots. This will give you a good indication of the direction the market is moving, and how your property is performing in comparison to other properties in the same market. Your Excel spreadsheet should be organized by year, and ideally, there should be a positive trend with the property you want to buy over time.

Tip 8: Buy Low Sell High (Invest in Emerging Neighborhoods)

Readers trained in the stock market will immediately notice this tip as emerging from buying stocks. Not only is this logic the name of the game on Wall Street, it is also best practices on Main Street. Real estate investing strategies take a lot from the stock market, and this tip is no exception. So how does the future real estate mogul 'buy low and sell high' in the real estate market? The trick is to look at emerging neighborhoods within urban areas. Imagine Harlem, New York in the 1970s. It was known as the ghetto, graffiti infested, harboring gangs, and with crumbling infrastructure. However, something has happened to Harlem over the past 15 years. Its proximity to Manhattan, combined with **gentrification**,[14] has increased property values immensely in the recent past. For the investor with an astute eye, investing in Harlem a few years ago could have paid dividends.

Harlem is not the only emerging neighborhood. The Bronx outside of Manhattan has experienced a similar revival; so has Manayunk in Philadelphia, Wynwood in Miami, city center Pittsburgh, and almost every neighborhood of San Francisco. When investing, take a look at emerging markets near your community to capitalize upon this strategy. In the words of the President of Home Qualified, Ralph DiBugnara, "rental properties represent a great way to get involved with real estate investments. Emerging neighborhoods offer growth potential and tax incentives for buyers. Buyers that purchase properties in emerging neighborhoods maximize profits and ensure that their income covers their costs" (Roofstock 2018).[15]

---

[14] Gentrification is a phenomenon by which wealthier individuals begin moving into poorer neighborhoods, thereby increasing property values. Gentrification is commonly known as an adverse symptom of economic development, as poor people do not become richer; rather they are forced to move out of their homes and look for rental units further and further from their jobs. Oftentimes in the United States, 'ghettos' have been created due to gentrified communities.

[15] Quotes from Ralph DiBugnara and Shawn Breyer taken from https://learn.roofstock.com/blog/real-estate-investing-tips-from-successful-investors.

Tip 9: Solve Maintenance Issues NOW!

Similar to healthcare, maintenance issues tend to get worse over time. Imagine that you have a cavity in one of your molars, but do not want to pay the $40 that the dentist charges to fill it. Over time, this cavity will grow, leading to greater tooth decay. Next time you visit your dentist, she says that it'll now take $80 to fill the cavity, as it's twice as big as before. Yet, you still do not want to pay for the filling. Pretty soon the entire tooth may need to be removed and you may need a root canal procedure that will set you back $1,000. A problem that could have been fixed with $40 at its outset now sets you back a grand. Maintenance issues are of a similar breed.

Tenants complaining that the air conditioning unit is leaking a little bit of water may seem like a simple nuisance at its genesis. However, that small amount of leaking can increase to more leaking, and before you know it, there is a veritable flood of water coming from the A/C unit and causing damage not only to your property, but someone else's property as well. Something that could have cost the investor a hundred dollars in A/C repairs can set them back thousands of dollars if they ignore the initial problem.

Tip 10: Have Multiple Exit Strategies

Properties may not attract tenants, may depreciate in value over time, may be destroyed by natural disasters, or may lose their value through wear and tear. The wise investor needs to know that not all properties will bring them a positive cash flow in the way they originally intended. If they believe that a property is a great rental unit, but nobody is interested in renting it, the investor may have to examine whether or not it is worth selling. Other properties may be excellent rental units, but due to the wear and tear of their appliances over time, they may not appreciate at the same rate as others in the same neighborhood. To hedge against these potentialities, the investor must always have multiple exit strategies.

Shawn Breyer, from Breyer Home Buyers offers an excellent example when discussing his strategy for flipping homes (buying foreclosed properties, remodeling them, and then selling them at a profit). He notes that if you are flipping a property "and the market tanks, but the property would be even or negative cash flow when rented out then you're most likely going to lose tens of thousands of dollars. Flipping starter homes that are in the price ranges that can be rented out for solid cash flow every month allows you to either build wealth by keeping them as rentals or mitigate your risks when things go sideways (Ibid.)." By having multiple ways to make money out of the properties you invest in, you are essentially not putting your eggs in one basket.

Tip 11: Ignore Your Emotions

The roots of this tip are actually found in Chapter 2, but it's worth investigating more into this issue. Investors time and again always put their emotions before the market, ignorant of the fact that the market does not care one iota for your emotions. Fear and greed are excellent ways to lose money in the real estate (and stock) market. The reason why so many people lose money in both markets is because their emotions override logic and rationality. There is a saying in Wall Street that denotes this phenomenon accurately: 'the bulls win, the bears win, but the pigs get slaughtered.' This means that those who think the market will rise (bulls) tend to make money, and those who think the market will drop (bears) also make money. So who loses? Those who invest out of emotion (the pigs). They're the ones that get slaughtered time and again. The same exact rules apply in the real estate market. Those who cannot stomach a short-term downslide in real estate values and sell out of desperation will always lose money.

When investing in real estate, do not simply trust your emotions. Take your time to do the homework and determine yield rates across similar properties (remember the 1% rent rule?). Also, do not underestimate insurance costs, taxes, and maintenance costs. All of these factors combined can erode away any profits you may be making from rent. Remember, your goal is to save enough money for your next property. The investor cannot hope to do this if all of the income from rents is taken up by maintenance and insurance costs.

Tip 12: Pay Down Debt Over Time

For the first few years of your real estate life, it is in your best interest to accrue more and more properties and rent them out to tenants. This will leave you with significant cash flow, but also significant debt. After a few years with constant and increasing cash flow, it is in your best interest to pay off the debt that has acrued on your properties. Here's the reason: in any mortgage statement, the interest is paid first and the principle is paid last. This means that the bank wants to make sure that you paid for their trust (remember where the word 'credit' comes from?) first, and then their loan second.[16] Along traditional loans, the only way to pay down your debt first, and deal with less interest last is to override the system. Instead of continuously paying down your debt along a 30-year period, you'd have to pay extra in bulk. This means that you would drop $10,000 in principle every year or so to pay down the debt.

Tools At Your Disposal

The first-time investor may feel very overwhelmed by the thought of dropping thousands of dollars on an investment, working day and night with tenants to barely make ends meet, and may know nothing of insurance companies or even where to find a home. Luckily there are multiple tools at your disposal where you can learn more about real estate investing. Some of these tools are

---

[16] As a side note, it's suggestive to note that banks are more concerned about how trustworthy you are before they think about how much money you have.

designed to help you pick properties, while others are geared toward improving your knowledge of real estate investing.

The first question many of the readers may be asking is where do they find a property? Whereas in the past, word of mouth, newspaper clippings, and physically driving around neighborhoods were how one found properties for sale, currently most of this is done on the Internet. The first website this book will analyze is Trulia (www.trulia.com). Once you're in the Trulia website, you can simply pick a city, town, or zip code to search for properties to rent, buy, or sell. This website lets the user search for homes by number of bathrooms, bedrooms, price ranges, square feet, lot size, and home types (houses, condos, townhomes, mobile homes, multi-family homes, and empty lots for future development). Over the past six months, Trulia has greatly improved their website design to include a map depicting where the property is located. Before this advancement, many investors had to use Google Maps to figure out the location of some properties. Trulia additionally offers interesting insight into crime rates, school rankings, and market trends.

The real estate data tracks the average price of a home in a city or zip code over the past ten years, depicting median price sales, percent changes, and so on. Trulia additionally allows the investor great insight into which *types* of homes appreciated over time and which did not, demarcating the homes into single-bedroom properties, double-bedroom properties, and so on. Crime data in Trulia is also sophisticatedly advanced. Trulia detects police CAD system alarms, denoting which areas tend to experience more violent crime, and plugs this information into the maps on their website. By using a similar technology, Trulia also shows which schools are performing better than others, ranking them on a scale from one to ten. Additionally, in August 2018, Trulia launched Trulia Neighborhoods, enabling homebuyers, sellers, and investors to get detailed information on a specific neighborhood. This feature has footage from drones, users' photographs, and the rankings of local restaurants and schools by the locals. This may provide a lot of valuable insight to the future investor, but Trulia is not the only website offering this type of information.

Zillow is Trulia's largest competitor (www.zillow.com). Up until recently, Zillow's main advantage was its maps. It was able to accurately locate properties and pin them on maps, while with Trulia, the investor had to use some other mapping software. Similar to Trulia, Zillow allows the future investor to search by address, city, or zip code. Also similar are the search options (number of bedrooms, number of bathrooms, property type, etc.).

Zillow does seem to have an advantage over Trulia in the details given in listing type of property. It allows the investor to search for homes for sale by agents, owners, new construction, foreclosures, and 'coming soon.' Furthermore, Zillow has a potential listings option, detailing foreclosed and pre-foreclosed properties. If Zillow and Trulia sound oddly similar it is because in

2014, Zillow bought Trulia for $3.5 billion while Trulia's co-founder and triathlete Sami Inkinen rowed across the Pacific for fun (Gelles 2014), [17] leading both websites to have the same properties available online with similar features.

Other than websites for finding properties, there are two that are useful for locating solid property management companies, the Institute of Real Estate Management (IREM), found at www.irem.org, and the National Association of Residential Property Managers' (NARPM) website, found at www.narpm.org. Let's start with IREM. They are an international force of nearly 20,000 individuals seeking to advance the property management industry. They provide training, professional development, and intuitive collaboration among their members, leading this organization to be quite robust among industry leaders. They have four different types of memberships: credentials, associate, student, and academic memberships.

The credentials membership is for asset and property managers for mostly residential and commercial properties. The associate membership is likely the type of membership the reader is interested in learning more about. This membership is for the investors themselves, where they can connect with those possessing a credentials membership. The associate membership automatically allows the investor to become part of the IREM

---

[17] Information taken from https://dealbook.nytimes.com/2014/07/29/trulias-co-founder-rows-across-ocean-even-as-company-is-sold-to-zillow/.

community and helps them make personal contacts and connections with reputable property management companies. Furthermore, becoming an associate gives the members discounts on IREM's publications and courses.

Some of the younger readers may be interested in student memberships. These are geared for full-time college students looking to enter the real estate management industry. Similar to the associate membership, they also gain access to discounted publications and courses. Finally, the academic membership is for those professors of real estate management topics at secondary and tertiary levels.

When the investor is looking for accredited property managers, the IREM website is of particular use. Not only does this website provide an up-to-date forum for property managers, it has courses offering those interested in property management accreditation. For example, the Certified Property Manager (CPM) course is one that allows people to receive their accreditation. For residential property managers new to the profession and seeking to become accredited, the Accredited Residential Manager (ARM) course is also available. Of particular note for the investor, a group with CPM or ARM at their end of their name allows the investor to immediately know that they are accredited either individually or as an agency. Not only does this bestow some degree of credibility, it allows for a tight-knit community to form across an otherwise disparate community.

Similar to IREM, the National Association of Residential Property Managers (NARPM) offers a community and courses for the investor. Of particular note is their convention that attracts investors, property management companies, moguls, and academics from across the country. In 2018, they celebrated their 30th annual convention and trade show, offering workshops and seminars on the industry. If there is any convention that this book suggests the investor should attend, it is NARPM's trade show and convention (usually held in October). NARPM also offers many resources regarding the legislative process, bureaucratic politics, and government regulation, which comes in especially useful in highly regulated states, such as Illinois and Pennsylvania. NARPM allows the investor to become more involved in their legislative process to help government and elected officials learn more about the nuances of property management so that they do not create regulations strangling your business. Every year, state legislatures around the country consider legislation regarding liability, affordable housing, and landlord/tenant relations. Uniting behind one voice, NARPM in this case, allows the investor to act as part of one bloc in a complex, long, and often frustrating legislative process.

NARPM also has a blog and newsletter, which keeps their members informed of changes in the property management industry. Similar to IREM, NARPM allows for the future investor to search for property management companies by name, address, zip code, housing type, and so on. NARPM guarantees that their members meet their ethics and rules guidelines, along with adhering to their standards of professionalism. Due to their communication with state legislators across the United States, NARPM furthermore helps members know important pending legislative items that affect their property. On a micro-level, their members are also knowledgeable about rent values, vacancy factors, and have heightened levels of expertise and industry knowledge to assist the investor. Along this vein, many NARPM members have already developed a community around their business, indicating that they can help tenants find electricians, plumbers, and carpenters to handle appliance and maintenance issues.

In addition to property management company websites, there are multiple blogs and podcasts that are popular among real estate investors. One of the most famous blogs is the Bigger Pockets podcast. One of my favorite things about this podcast is that the investor does not have to subscribe to their channel in order to download the information. Their data is up online at www.biggerpockets.com. This blog, podcast, and website combines an incredible amount of data into one specific place. It allows for the investor to learn about the nuances of different property management companies, tax law, rural and urban investing, and much more.

Another benefit of Bigger Pockets is that it is an ongoing blog and podcast, making it 'organic.' It can change depending upon changes in the market. Because this podcast and blog is not static, it effectively acts like a news source for the real estate market. In the same way someone who is interested in world events would watch BBC, the investor interested in real estate investment should tune in to Bigger Pockets. There is a caveat here: the fact that this blog and podcast discusses current events in the real estate market may lead many investors to rush to one aspect of the market over another. Sometimes, especially when it comes to emerging neighborhoods, it is sometimes better to go against the grain and not follow the mass of investors into one arena. As always, prudence should be used when investing in future properties.

Now that the reader has a hint of the tools out their (most of which are completely free), it is imperative to understand the people involved in the real estate game. Oftentimes, managing clients, securing tenants, and dealing with property management companies can save the investor thousands of dollars and endless headaches. The next chapter will discuss how to be a good landlord, how to retain tenants and keep a mentor, and how to address your finances. All of these elements, combined with the knowledge that you learned from the previous chapters, should give you a decent introduction into the real estate market.

CHAPTER 4: YOUR PEOPLE AND ACCOUNTS

As alluded to in the previous chapters, one of the most important tools that the future investor needs to have is a community. But what does this mean? For the mogul, a 'community' is a group of interested people in the real estate market. This community includes tenants, realtors, other competitors, property management companies, and a mentor. We have briefly touched upon the situations on where to find adequate property management companies, but how does the investor go about determining to whom they should rent their property? The junior investor sometimes gets caught up in the system of real estate investing that they forget to vet out their tenants. Below are some suggestions to make sure that you attract the right type of tenants for your properties.

First and foremost, the investor should *interview* the potential tenant, or get the property management company to do the work for them. This does not have to be a formal interview, but a general meeting so that the investor knows the economic situation the tenant possesses. While it may not be necessary to run a background or credit check, it is useful to know if they have a job and can pay rent every month. The worst situation for the landlord is eviction. This process takes a long time, the investor loses money, the tenant is left without a home, and 'word of mouth' can damage the reputation of the business you are trying to build. For example, interviewing college students would give the investor a basic idea of what to expect in terms of the short length of time the tenant will stay in the property. On the other hand, a retired couple looking to stay in an apartment is much more likely to occupy a property for many years. Interviewing, in a very informal sense, is the best way to gauge which way the wind is blowing for a specific property.

Knowing your property is key to maintaining the right types of tenants. In essence, the investor must know that maintaining the right tenants is contingent upon the type of property they own. If it's a 55+ community, you likely do not want Millennials occupying a home for an extended period of time, or want parents with small children running in the streets. Properties located close to universities should expect to receive more college and graduate level students than those in rural communities far away from higher education campuses.

An apartment in a big city may generate varying different types of tenants contingent upon the neighborhood it is located in. Especially in urban regions (and some towns whose real estate acts like a microcosm of urban centers), a heterogeneous population of tenants may benefit the investor. If they have multiple-family housing, a combination of Millennials, empty-nesters, and retired folks may be beneficial to keeping tenants. However, using the same logic, this would not be the case in a rural setting. The general rule of thumb here is to know your property. If you know it well enough, you can predict the type of tenants you will receive, and by extension, retain them for as long as possible.

Now that the investor has 'interviewed' the tenants and knows the strengths/weaknesses of their properties, they can begin acting as a landlord (or, in the case of multi-family properties, subcontract this out to a property management company). The first step to being a good landlord is facilitating what I call the 'processing part' of recruiting tenants. Inundating future tenants with endless paperwork at the beginning of their experience with you, the landlord, or the property management company, leaves a sour taste in most tenants' mouths. Limiting the required paperwork to 'simple English' immediately gives the tenants a solid first impression and depicts how efficient you are as a landlord. Limiting paperwork additionally makes the investor's life easier, as part of this requires mediating between the investor and other insurance groups.

The second suggestion that every landlord should work on to ensure that their tenants remain in their units is to address concerns immediately. Generally speaking, tenants do not raise concerns that are not existent. If they do, the investor probably did a poor job in vetting the prospective tenant. As hinted in the tips and tricks section of Chapter 3, small problems end up becoming big problems over time. These larger problems not only destroy the property one owns, they erode away tenants, and damage your reputation as an investor. As was seen with the dentist example in

Chapter 3, it is better to spend a little bit of money now than to pay a lot of money later.

Here's the fundamental problem with most investors: they do not view their tenants as partners. The wise investor understands that if they are to generate passive income off of their investments, their tenants are not only their clients, but also their partners. Without them, the investor *loses* money, as they still have to swallow the costs of the mortgage without incoming revenues from rental properties. Clients help one make money, but only partners can *lose* money for the investor. Treating tenants as replaceable or expendable will ultimately lead to an increase in turnover and lost revenue on your properties.

Now that the future investor has an adequate idea of how to retain tenants over extended periods of time, it is incumbent upon the author to discuss the importance of a mentor. We touched upon this topic a few chapters ago, but the essence of a mentor is significant enough that we must delve into this in more detail. There are many 'keys' to being a successful investor, but one of these is to have a mentor. Before we begin on how a mentor can help the future mogul, we must ask ourselves: where do we find a mentor? There are many places for this, and rest assured, you may find yours in the most unlikely of places. Mentors can usually be found in real estate conferences. These venues are excellent networking places to meet other investors, glean knowledge from property management companies, and talk to those who have made (and lost) a lot of money in the real estate game. Additionally, mentors may be found speaking to your landlord, your homeowners association, or even at colleges and universities.

The proper mentor will not necessarily teach you what to do in certain situations (you have to figure that out for yourself). Rather, good mentors allow the future investor to learn from their mistakes. Oftentimes, these mistakes make for better stories. Mentors have in-depth knowledge about certain regions that may help the future investor. Additionally, they are, more than anyone else, experts in a specific type of property. The reader will hopefully remember Tip 1 stating that they should specialize. Finding the right mentor that knows enough about a type of apartment complex or single-family home will help the future investor greatly.

In addition to parting with knowledge, they may know specific contractors that specialize in a type of appliance, HOA management style, and so on. It is also worth noting that the first few years of the investor's life in the real estate industry can feel like a roller coaster. When the times are down and the investor is losing hope, a mentor can step in and keep you aligned and in decent spirits. The opposite is also true, of course. When the money is rolling in and you feel on top of the world, do not forget the lessons of humility and hard work that your mentor will impart upon you. Many moguls forget this aspect of real estate investing, finding to their detriment that when the bad times come, they have neither money nor a mentor to guide them.

Managing Your Finances

Now that you have your community squared away, it's important to manage your finances correctly. This section is designed to illustrate ideal practices for managing your finances. Remember, the two ways to make money in real estate investing are through tenants' rents and the appreciation of your home. While the investor does not have complete control over the income received from their investments, they have more control over rents than property appreciation. With this in mind, there are a few pointers that the investor should be aware of when it comes to managing cash flow.

As the reader will recall, there is a general 1% rent rule, whereby the rent charged per month is one percent of the value of the property. So a $150,000 home should incur around $1,500 in rent every month. Keep in mind that the difference between rents and expenses is the cash flow. Now here's where we are adding to the general rule: rent should be one-third more than the value of the mortgage for the home *and* simultaneously at least one percent of the total value of the home. While the 1% rule is simply the way things turn out for many properties, it is not a hard and fast rule for the investor. Because we are adding another variable to this equation, let's use an example.

Rebecca is buying a home for $200,000 in Maine, and is looking to rent it out to Tom and Susan. Now Rebecca was able to put $50,000 as a down payment, which is 25% of the total amount of the home, not the usual 20%. Now Rebecca's mortgage is $150,000. This equates to around $416 a month on the mortgage itself, plus property and school taxes, interest, and maintenance on the home. Let's imagine that all of these variables together set her back $2,100 a month, which is a common-sized mortgage for such a home in many US states. She is familiar with the one percent rule and understands that generally, her property should get about $2,000 in rent monthly, but sees that her expenses are at $2,100. Rebecca is also interested in growing her passive income and not simply treading water.

So, what should she charge Tom and Susan per month? Well, she needs to follow two rules, the one percent rule and the 1/3 value of the mortgage rule. She is already above the one percent threshold with her mortgage, so she's going to have to add one-third of $2,100 to her total rent, thereby charging Tom and Susan $2,800 per month. For Rebecca, this covers her mortgage ($2,100), satisfies the 1% rent rule ($2,000), and leaves her $700 for savings for her future property. If she has a job, she should be using that active income for any large deposits in improving her home.

The reader will remember that the only way to make large sums of money on the real estate market are through saving revenue from your previous property to add as the down payment for the next property.[18] This means that the $700 that Rebecca saved per month should *not* go into the same pot as her general personal expenses covering her food, travel, and medical expenses. In order to keep some semblance of discipline, Rebecca should not put her revenue from rental properties in the same pot as her active income. By separating passive income off her properties from any type of active income, she can keep better control of her finances. What she does not want is any mixture of active and passive incomes. This commingling of incomes renders it difficult to separate the values and percentages of income from passive and active sources. It would be like pouring a bucket of water into a river and hoping to pick up the same water downstream. The same holds true for tenants' rents: never mix up the revenue generated from one tenant with the revenue generated from another. Should a mistake occur, this is a headache to undo, and it allows the investor to clearly glean information from their cash flow spreadsheet.

Now that the reader knows how to calculate property values and estimate rent for tenants, we must talk about taxes. For many, taxes are a sour aspect of real estate investing, as many investors do not see their value. However, your taxes go to ensure roads exist and are taken care of when you're driving to your

---

[18] It is always difficult to raise rents on tenants, so it is oftentimes better to charge a little more at the outset rather than having to change tenants' rents every year to make ends meet. This will furthermore keep turnover low.

property. They cover infrastructure costs for bridges and tunnels. They pay for police, fire, and EMS services should there be an emergency. Taxes also pay for schools. The reader will likely remember that when an investor is looking for a property, they search for places where there is little crime and solid schools – your taxes are the price you pay for those accommodations. While the investor does not directly benefit from taxes, there are plenty of indirect benefits, ranging from better schools to safer bridges. Now that we (unwillingly) understand why properties are taxed, here is how the investor can calculate their monthly costs.

The first step in calculating property taxes is determining the value of the property. Usually this is done at the county level by a property appraiser. This 'assessor' determines what the cost of the home is and can judge what the taxes are for each property. While the assessed value of the home is oftentimes similar to the price the investor pays for the home, it is usually not an exact science. A safe bet is that the property will not be assessed at either 10% higher or lower than the purchasing price of the property. While this information is publicly available, there are private institutions that assess the value of your home as well.[19] Most assessors incorporate the value of the land into your property value, so make sure to include this variable as part of your total

---

[19] For example, Chase Bank offers a free Home Value Estimator that can be found at their website here: https://www.chase.com/mortgage/mortgage-resources/home-value-estimator.

calculation of your property value. The second step is to obtain any improvements the investor has done to their home (hardwood flooring, upgraded kitchen and bath, etc.), and add that number to the property value of the home. So if Lawrence bought a home for $150,000, his land value is estimated at $40,000, and he added another $10,000 of improvements to his home, then his total property value is $200,000.

Now that the investor knows the total value of the home, they must find out the local government's tax rate. Most tax rates are determined at a value called 'per **mill**' or per $1,000 of assessed value. So if a tax rate is considered to be 20 mills, it is essentially taxing 2% of the total value of your home. These 'mills' are used by local, state, and town authorities to tax properties within their jurisdiction. For most regions of the United States, the local authority that will take the heaviest tax on your property is the county. However, in some places, such as Connecticut, Pennsylvania, and New Jersey, boroughs and townships carry a lot of the tax burdens instead of the counties. Once the investor receives all of the county (and depending where the property is located, sub-county) taxes, they can estimate the total taxed value of their property simply by adding up the mills.

Let's suppose that Armando's property in Florida is estimated at $300,000 including land and home renovations. If he lives in Lake County, and their property assessor determines that they have a tax rate of 20 mills, Armando knows that they are taxing 2% of their property. Additionally, the small town his property is located in levies another 10 mills (one percent) of property taxes. Simply by adding up the two taxes together, 30 mills or three percent, Armando knows that his home will be taxed at 3% of 300,000, or $9,000 annually. The smart investor will always calculate this figure before buying a property and before renting it out to tenants.

The final calculation to be made is determining the insurance cost of your home. As an investor, you only really need to cover dwelling insurance, and not worry about possession insurance. That is usually the responsibility of the tenant and is contingent upon their valuables and possessions. **Dwelling insurance**, also called dwelling coverage, is part of a standard insurance policy covering the value of your home in case of fire, flood, and other natural disasters. There are multiple property insurance calculators on the market that can supply an investor with a quick figure based off only a few factors. For example, Home Insurance.com (www.homeinsurance.com) has a calculator that gives the investor a rough estimate of insurance costs. The only information the investor must provide is the zip code (all property values are different per zip code) and square footage of the property. With these two bits of information, this company can provide an accurate estimate of the insurance value for your property.

Expenses:

A classic mistake the rookie real estate investor makes is overlooking or underestimating expenses that they will incur on their investment. In a perfect world, you could buy a rental property, collect rent every month, pay your mortgage taxes and insurance and pocket the rest, but in reality, it's never quite that simple. Expenses are about as unavoidable as taxes. If you're planning on holding a property for the life of the mortgage, you're talking 15-30 years. You're going to be putting aw significant amount of money into maintaining and updating the house so it doesn't fall into disrepair. If you want your house to appreciate in value and if you want to keep good tenants, you have to make sure that it stays a nice place to live.

For example, the roof will probably need to be replaced at some point. That could be an easy $5-10,000. At some point you'll need to update the heating and cooling units. You'll need to update the basement weather-proofing, perhaps you'll redo the driveway. Eventually you may want to redo the bathrooms and/or kitchen to keep the house modern and up to date. With a plan in place and with careful saving, these expenses don't need to eat a hole in your profits. The smart investor will factor these expenses into his numbers before even making the investment. These expenses should be considered a cost of doing business.

You should see these expenses as fixed just like your mortgage—a certain amount of money you have to pay out every month.

So how do you plan for this? Typically, there are fixed expenses and variable expenses. The **fixed expenses** are usually utilities which may be paid all or in part by the tenant. This includes: water, sewage, electricity, gas, trash etc. Depending on your agreement with your tenant, any of these expenses that the tenant is not agreeing to pay will fall on your shoulders. You should also be aware that if the property is vacant, you will have to pay these fees or else have the utilities disabled temporarily.

Variable expenses are expenses that change from month to month. These are typically repairs and cannot be predicted, but generally, follows a trajectory so that you're spending about the same amount each year. This includes plumbing emergencies, electrical issues etc. You may spend a lot one month and then nothing the next month. For example, if a pipe bursts and you have to call an emergency plumber, you may incur $500 in expenses this month. But next month, you may have $0 repair costs. You'll want to look at the overall year and set aside a certain amount of the rent income each month to cover any repair expenses that arise. A general rule of thumb is to set aside 5-10% of your rent income for repair (or variable) expenses.

The third type of expense is **Capital expense**. These aren't so much repairs as "investments" into the property. Updates and improvements to increase the value of the property and to ensure that your home appreciates. As mentioned earlier, this can include renovations, replacing the roof or driveway, updating amenities etc. These types of expenses are irregular and won't be incurred every month or even every year, but you should still be setting aside rental income each month so that you can fund them without having to use your personal funds. This one is a little bit harder to predict, and part of it will depend on the type of property you buy. You should, of course, have it inspected and try to estimate how much will need to be done throughout the term that you hold the property. The Bigger Pockets website says that a good estimate is 5-7% of your rental income. Of course, some years, you won't use these funds at all, but other years you will use everything you've saved and then some. A good investment plan is all about mitigating your financial risk and planning for any situation.

Another expense you will have to consider is Property Management. If you're planning on managing your own properties, then you don't have to worry about this. However, if you want this to be a fairly passive investment and you don't want to have to deal with every property emergency or tenant inquiry, then you may want to consider a property management company. You can read more about how to find a good property management company and what to look for in the Property Management section, but in terms of expenses, Property Management Companies typically charge 10% of your rent. So if you're using Property Management, you'll want to factor this into your numbers as well.

To determine **true cash flow**, you'll want to deduct all the expenses, mortgage, insurance and tax from your rental income. So if we go back to the example of Thomas who charges $1800 per month and has $800/month mortgage that includes taxes and insurance, now we will also need to subtract his property management, variable and capital expenses to determine his true cashflow.

Gross Rent: $1800

-Mortgage/Insurance/Taxes:-$800

-Variable Expenses (~7%)-126

-Capital Expenses (~7%)-126

-Property Management Expenses (10%)-180

TRUE CASH FLOW: $568

So, you can see the true cashflow is almost half of what you may have initially thought once you factor in all the other expenses. It looks like Thomas's expenses (not counting Mortgage, Tax, and Insurance) would be around $432. So you take the total gross rent income: $1800, subtract total expenses of $1232 ($800 for mortgage tax and insurance + $432 for Total other expenses) and you'll get the true cashflow amount of $568 per month.

Please note that this is just a simple example. Each rental situation is different and the numbers may need to be adjusted accordingly. For example, your variable costs may need to be higher if its an older house that has more frequent need of repairs. It also doesn't factor in any type of utility cost because this example assumes that the tenant pays all the utilities. However, if you have an agreement with the tenant where you pay some part of the utilities, you'll have to add that to your fixed expenses. Also, if there are Home Owner Association fees or any other type of monthly fee, make sure to include these in your numbers.

If Thomas decided to go without the Property Management company, he'd be able to reduce his costs by up to 10% increasing his true cash flow up to $748/month. But he will have significantly more responsibility with the property and will be responsible for handling all tenant inquiries and issues. This is a consideration you'll have to make. If you aren't a particularly handy person and don't want to be very actively involved in managing this property, it will likely be worth the price to hire a good property management company that you trust. If you're a handy person that lives near the rental property and you have good tenants and a stable property, you may do just fine going without a property management company. (There are plenty of people that even own properties from out of state that don't use property management companies. It all just depends on your particular situation.) You will want to keep in mind your long-term goal of holding a large portfolio of properties. When you get beyond a few properties, it may be exceedingly difficult to do all the property management yourself. A possible strategy is to do the management yourself for the first few properties to maximize your cashflow, then once you get past a certain number of properties, start using property managers for all your properties so you can focus your time and efforts on maximizing profits and increasing your portfolio.

These examples and guidelines are more geared to single-family or small multi-family properties. For larger multi-family properties (5+ units) you'll definitely want to have a property management company, but the good news is that you'll be able to control and predict your expenses more profitably. One of the biggest advantages of multi-family properties is their uniformity and composition of being part of one big property. For example, when a roof needs replaced, you'll likely need to fix one big roof that goes over the entire apartment complex—not 40 individual single-family roofs. Your savings in such a scenario will be exponential. That's the long-term goal. To really make real cash-flow—the type of cash-flow where you can quit your job and live off your investments, you'll want to move towards the goal of larger multi-family properties once you accumulate the capital for the down payment.

CHAPTER 5: ALTERNATIVE WAYS TO INVEST & CONCLUSION

The majority of this book deals with investing in single and multi-family real estate properties, but there are other types of investments that this section will touch upon. We will not delve into too many specifics as it is not the focus of this book, but it is important to note how these alternative ways to invest may help diversify your real estate portfolio. The first option is commercial real estate.

Commercial real estate are those properties where people work and do not live in, such as office buildings, warehouses, medical offices, and retail space. Similar to residential investing, the two ways to earn money in commercial real estate are through rents and appreciation. If you do not have a lot of capital, a good strategy to investing in commercial real estate is to begin small and work your way up. Laundry services in apartment buildings, vending machines in office buildings, and the like, are small types of commercial real estate investing that do not require much overhead costs.

One of the benefits of commercial real estate is that their rates of appreciation are generally much higher than residential rates, sometimes reaching double digits. Additionally, when an investor puts money in commercial properties, they have the opportunity to network with the commercial enterprise and build professional relationships. Other benefits of investing in commercial real estate are that their hours of operation are during the day, meaning that the investor can rest easy at night, and there are more objective price evaluations of the property.

On the downside, commercial real estate tends to require much higher up-front costs. But the investor can expect higher capital returns. However, your property "might be humming along for a few months and wham, here comes a $10,000 bill to address roofing repairs or a new furnace. With more customers there are more facilities to maintain and therefore more costs" (Larson 2018).[20] Larson also mentions that when dealing with commercial real estate, the time commitment tends to be higher if you are investing without a property management company. Multiple leases, public safety concerns, and maintenance issues all rise up stronger in commercial real estate than in residential investing. Along this vein, because commercial real estate is viewed as a wealthier enterprise, some scrupulous people may slip on ice or fall down a stairway and attempt to sue your LLC or LLP. In this sense, commercial real estate investing is riskier than residential investing because people generally do not spray paint or vandalize homes, and don't try to sue tenants.

---

[20] Information taken from https://www.nolo.com/legal-encyclopedia/pros-cons-investing-commercial-real-estate.html.

Creative Funding & Loans

The first type of non-standard loan is called an **FHA Loan**. These are loans insured by the Federal Housing Administration (FHA). These loans are unique and popular for first-time investors with little capital because they do not require the usual 20% down payment. Rather, these loans allow for a 3.5% down payment if the investor's credit score is above 580. If the investor's credit score is hovering between 500 and 579, then they will have to pay 10% as part of the down payment. The flip side of these unnaturally low down payments is that the monthly interest rate is higher for each property. The United States developed the FHA program in response to "the rash of foreclosures and defaults that happened in 1930s; to provide mortgage lenders with adequate insurance; and to help stimulate the housing market by making loans accessible and affordable for people with less than stellar credit or a low down payment" (Zillow 2018).[21] The basic notion is that the federal government insures the FHA loans to reduce their risks should the investor default on paying down their mortgage.

The benefits of an FHA loan is that since the down payment is so low in comparison to standard loans, college students in their early 20s with little capital can afford to buy their first property and take the first step to becoming a real estate investor. However, this type of loan requires mortgage insurance. Because the FHA,

---

[21] Information taken from https://www.zillow.com/mortgage-learning/fha-loan/.

which is a department of the United States, does not trust the investor yet, they need to buy mortgage insurance. There are two ways to gain the trust (remember this word is 'credit' in Latin, which is where the term comes from) of the US government: obtain more capital or have better credit. Here's the catch: if the investor has enough capital, they don't need an FHA loan, and if they had great credit, they could obtain a regular loan. So until the government considers the investor trustworthy, they will charge mortgage insurance.

There are two types of mortgage insurance: up-front insurance premiums and annual MIPs. The up-front insurance premium is a one-time payment, whereby investors pay a premium of 1.75% of the home loan. Usually, this payment is part of the settlement cost when an investor buys a home. Alternatively, this cost can be rolled into the mortgage. The other option is an annual MIP (mortgage insurance payment), which, confusingly enough, is paid monthly. In these cases, the "amount of the mortgage insurance premium is a percentage of the loan amount, based on the borrower's loan-to-value (LTV) ratio, loan size, and length of loan" (Ibid.). There are also federal limits on the value of the property that can be bought with an FHA loan, usually hovering in the $600,000 to $700,000 range. Further restrictions depend on the state and county the property is located in, so these factors may need to be accounted for in future investments.

The investor should know that FHA loans are meant for those individuals seeking to buy only one home. If you are to be a real estate mogul, you normally cannot buy a second or third property with an FHA loan. However, if you are interested in multi-family real estate investments, but do not have the capital necessary for a 20% down payment, you can take on an FHA loan and rent out the other bedrooms and bathrooms to tenants. If this is the route you choose to take, make sure to account for the extra mortgage insurance costs and higher interest rates into the rents for your future tenants. Breaking even in an FHA loan is not a good situation to be in because not only may the investor lose money, their credit score may drop, and they may get backlogged on interest payments for their home.

Another option for the future mogul is a **hard money loan**. Unlike traditional loans that are interested in whether or not an investor is trustworthy, hard money loans lend capital based on **collateral** securing the loan. Because hard money loans are contingent upon collateral (the asset you put forth to show your creditworthiness), they are less interested in whether or not the investor can repay the loan. The collateral takes care of that. Should the investor prove incapable of repaying the loan, the borrower must forfeit the collateral. Hard money loans are riskier in this sense, because if the collateral is a property, there is no way for *part* of the property to be forfeited. They are additionally known for being short-term loans as interest rates for hard money loans tend to be higher than standard loans.

If hard money loans initially sound like they belong in a loan shark movie, you are half correct. So what are the benefits of hard money loans? First is speed. Because these loans are based off of collateral, lenders are largely uninterested in whether or not the borrower can repay the loan. Because of this, they do not bother with credit checks, long applications, reviewing credit card statements, and the like.

Of particular note, the speed by which hard money loans are arranged increase with each subsequent loan. Since the company knows that the borrower is good for their money, the process speeds up with every subsequent loan. As Pritchard notes, "once you have a relationship with a lender, the process can move quickly, giving you the ability to close deals that others can't close (that's especially important in hot markets with multiple offers)" (Pritchard 2018). [22] Furthermore, because most hard money companies have loan-to-value (LTV) ratios that are pretty low (usually around 60%), they know that the property the borrower has put up as collateral can be sold quickly. This gives the lender more confidence, as they see that they could get their money back should the borrower default on the loan.

Hard money loans usually do not make sense for the first-time investor or for those who are interested in holding a property for a long period of time. If you are interested in purchasing a property and renting it out to tenants, a hard money loan is *not* for you. However, there is a very valuable place for them in the market.

---

[22] Information taken from https://www.thebalance.com/hard-money-basics-315413.

If an investor is looking to finance a fixer-upper, whereby they will buy a foreclosed home, repair it, and sell it at a higher price, then a hard money loan makes sense. Because of the speed associated with these loans, the investor can purchase the foreclosed property before other investors, take on a higher interest rate while the property is being upgraded, and repay the loan as the property is sold to the highest bidder.

Another real estate agreement worth investigating is **seller financing**, also known as owner financing or purchase-money mortgages. In such agreements, the seller of the property handles the mortgage process rather than a financial institution doing so on behalf of the purchaser. In these cases, instead of applying for a mortgage through a financial institution or a bank, the buyer and seller get together to sign the mortgage. The popularity of seller financing works in an indirect relationship with the stock market. According to Investopedia (2018),[23] during times when "banks are risk-averse and reluctant to lend money to any but the most credit-worthy borrowers, seller financing can make it possible for many more people to buy homes. [...] Conversely, when credit markets are loose, and banks are enthusiastically loaning money, seller financing has less appeal." In essence seller financing is a solid choice if the market is acting in a specific way congruent with your purchasing and investment goals.

---

[23] Investopedia is a solid source on a whole host of information relating to the real estate market, stocks, bonds, and leveraging debt. The quote above can be found at https://www.investopedia.com/terms/s/seller-financing.asp

There are some advantages and disadvantages to seller financing. Similar to hard money loans, the closing process is much faster with seller financing than with conventional loans. Additionally, because the seller is doing most of the work, there are little closing costs, as realtors, lawyers, and real estate companies are left out of the process. Generally, those with poor credit will gravitate to seller financing due to the low down payment to this type of agreement. However, the converse is also important. Seller financing options generally charge much higher interest rates than conventional loans. This is the chief drawback to this type of financing. The reason why banks and financial institutions can afford to charge such small percentages on interest rates is because they can afford to spread their risk across thousands of properties. When it comes to seller financing, there is only one property holding all of the risk, hence the higher interest rate.

The final 'different' way of investing in real estate is through real estate investment trusts (REIT). REITs are companies that own and (oftentimes) operate passive income generating real estate. The possibility of REITs date back to 1960, when Dwight D. Eisenhower signed into law the REIT Act title of the Cigar Excise Tax that was passed by Congress. REITs allowed investors to purchase highly diversified residential and commercial properties, but they didn't take off until a few years later. Originally modeled after mutual funds from the 1980s, REITs are exchange-traded funds (ETF) that allow the investor the chance to own valuable real estate and access dividend-based income and returns. In this sense,

REIT offers a theoretical middle ground in between the real estate and stock market. It allows the investor to put their money in real estate companies through the REIT, but since this is traded on stock exchanges as ETFs, they act like miniature mutual funds. REIT investors earn a share of income purchased through their investment without having to go out and physically purchase a home.

The REIT business model is worth examining. REITs are companies that lease out office buildings, apartment complexes, townhomes, warehouses and the like, and then collect rent on their real estate. This is how the company generates income, which is then paid out to its investors in the form of **dividends**.[24] By law, REITs must pay out at least 90% of their taxable income to shareholders, with many REITs paying out 100% of this income. Precisely because REITs are so diversified, the investor is purchasing real estate, yet the risk is spread out through multiple properties. The reader will note how this is a drastically different approach than many other real estate investments, where the risk is internalized into one property at a time.

There are multiple types of REITs. The most common type is an Equity REIT, which is a publicly traded equity stock. These types of assets are further broken down into geographic-specific, industry-specific, and commercial-specific types of REITs. For

---

[24] A dividend is money paid on a regular basis (often quarterly) by a company to shareholders out of its profits.

example, an REIT focusing only on farmland exists (stock ticker: LAND); another one focusing only on advertising real estate, such as billboards is available (ticker: LAMR); HST focuses only on hotels and lodging; SUI and UMH focus on manufactured housing; and multiple REITs focus on geographic regions of the world. Since REITs act as mutual funds in the stock market, they can typically be bought through financial services companies, such as E-Trade, Vanguard, and Fidelity. Keep in mind that many of these financial services companies have their own in-house REITs that can be bought without a service fee. For example, Vanguard's REIT covers office buildings and hotels, and can be bought without the investor incurring a service charge (stock ticker: VNQ). These REITs are often viewed as safer than many other types of investments in the stock market because they are diversified across multiple real estate investments.

Finally, because REITs are passively managed, in the sense that you do not need a stockbroker to do the work for you because you are doing it yourself, their **expense ratios** tend to be lower than many actively managed funds. An expense ratio is the amount, usually a percentage, charged to manage the account. Some financial management companies have high expense ratios because there are an army of stockbrokers and analysts seeking out higher returns on your investments. You pay them out through these expense ratios, which often hover within the 1-2% range. On the other hand, passively managed accounts, such as most REITs, have lower expense ratios, hovering at the 0.1-0.2% range. This means that with passively managed accounts, the investor can take home a higher percentage of the invested money. The downside to this reality is that since the investor does not have a stockbroker, they have to keep a sharp eye on their REIT investments.

CONCLUSION

This book covers a lot of territory, but the common theme throughout most of the work is that in order to succeed in real estate investment, you need to have a mindset as if you are playing Monopoly. Purchasing one property and renting it out to a tenant may seem like a lucrative investment for a time, but the reality is that the investor cannot possibly live off of one tenant. Just like Monopoly, the investor must save the money gained from their first tenant and use it as a down payment for their next property. This is where most investors get stuck. Lack of discipline, emergencies, and a desire for a more comfortable life tend to erode away the steadfast determination necessary to invest in a second property. It is so temptingly easy to begin to use one's first tenant's rent as a source of supplemental income rather than saving it for another property. If this book cautions against any type of behavior, this is it.

Rather, the wise real estate investor not only purchases a second and third property, but ten or twenty more. Only after purchasing this number of properties can an investor truly live off of their investments and not have an active income, such as a job. This book clearly favors multi-family properties as a viable investment. Multi-family real estate investments, more than anything else, bestow the investor with the benefits of economies of scale. Instead of having to drive around to multiple single-family properties with different management companies in different zip codes, the investor possessing a multi-family property enjoys all of their units having the same code, taxes, regulations, appliances, location, and down payment. All of the parts that make real estate investing difficult for single-family properties are eliminated for multi-family investments, rendering this a viable alternative for the future mogul. Of course, the difficulty in securing a loan for a multi-family property, combined with high up-front costs, render this alternative impractical for many investors at *present*. In the future, this should be a logical goal for many up-and-coming investors. By beginning with single-family homes and transitioning to multi-family properties as soon as possible, the investor could become a real estate mogul in less than a decade.

In order to reach this threshold, the future investor ought to understand the two large rules of cash flow for their properties. First, any rent charged to a tenant must be over the one percent rent rule, whereby the monthly rent supersedes at lease one percent the price of the property, *and* the investor should charge one-third more than the mortgage necessary to pay for the home. That extra one-third is then invested into the next property, and so on. The same logic applies for multi-family homes, which can generate a lot more capital for the investor at a faster rate than dozens of single-family homes. The goal for the real estate mogul should be to reach this level, the Big Leagues, of real estate investing, at the fastest pace possible.

This is how real estate moguls build their empires and become wealthier. They may have outsized personalities and eccentric ways of behaving, but deep down inside, they are very disciplined individuals who value the effort placed in real estate investing. Learning from the current giants will teach the future investor many of the more nuanced and theoretical tips and tricks not found in this book. To those seeking to embark upon the real estate ride, here is my final advice. Instead of focusing on location, location, location, as most investors suggest, perhaps what you should strive for is discipline, discipline, and discipline.

GLOSSARY

Active Appreciation Strategies: additions and renovations to one's property that increase its value, often coming in the form of bathroom and kitchen remodeling.

Active Income: any monetary gain that the investor must work for (e.g., a job).

Appreciation: also known as capital appreciation; an economic term illustrating how the value of an investment can increase over time.

Bots: short for robots; known for artificially manipulating the stock market.

Capital Expenses: A portion of money you set aside from your rental income each month to save for long-term improvements, maintenance and updates to the house over the life of the mortgage to ensure tenant satisfaction and property appreciation.

Capital Gains Tax (CGT): a tax levied on the increased value of sold good or securities.

Cash Flow Income: a form of passive income stemming from an investor's real estate assets whereby tenants pay the investor rent.

Collateral: something pledged as security for repayment of a loan, to be forfeited in the event of a default.

Credit Score: also called credit rating; a numeric number somewhere between the ranges of 250 to 850, depending on the credit bureau conducting the research.

Credit: stems from the Latin word for belief or trust; allows a financial institution to provide a borrower with capital without the borrower having to reimburse the institution immediately; opposite of debit.

Debt: the flip side of credit; the money that the borrower owes the creditor.

Depreciation: also known as capital depreciation; an economic term illustrating how the value of an investment can decrease over time.

Dividend: money paid on a regular basis (often quarterly) by a company to shareholders out of its profits.

Down Payment: also called deposits; payments used to purchase large assets, usually cars and homes.

Dwelling Insurance: also called dwelling coverage; part of a standard insurance policy covering the value of a property in case of fire, flood, and other natural disasters.

Economies of Scale: the cost advantages that investments receive due to their scale, whereby the cost of each additional unit of investment decreases with every increase in the number of units.

Empty Nester: reference to parents whose children have grown up and left home, leaving their original property comparably empty.

Exchange-Traded Fund (ETF): a security or stock that tracks an index, commodity, or basket of assets rather than a single stock.

Expense Ratio: the amount, usually a percentage, charged to manage a financial account, such as a stock, mutual fund, or ETF.

Fixed Expenses: Regular monthly fees incurred with your rental property including the mortgage, insurance, tax, Home Owner's Association Fees, and utilities (such as Water/sewage, trash, electricity, gas). Some of these fees may be paid by the tenant, but any that are not paid by the tenant must be factored into the investors monthly expenses.

Fixed Interest Loan: also called a fixed interest rate; a loan where the interest rate does not change.

Fixer-upper: often-foreclosed property that an investor buys at a discount from a bank, fixes them up, and then resells them for a profit.

Floating Interest Loan: also called a variable interest loan or an adjustable rate; lending where the interest on capital varies over time according to market adjustments.

Gentrification: a phenomenon by which wealthier individuals begin moving into poorer neighborhoods, thereby increasing property values.

Hard Money Loan: an asset-based loan through which an investor receives funds secured by collateral.

Inflation: phenomenon when there is a increase in the value of goods and services in an economy over time.

Interest: formerly labeled usury in the Middle Ages; the amount of capital the bank or financial institution charges for lending the borrower capital.

Leveraging: called gearing in Great Britain and Australia; the use of borrowed capital, such as a property, to increase the potential return on investment.

Limited Liabilities Company (LLC): companies that absorb liability costs from investments while leaving the entrepreneur or CEO's personal finances out of its jurisdiction.

Limited Liabilities Partnership (LLP): a company that allows the investor to share liabilities among other partners in your company, rendering it a safer alternative than LLCs.

Liquidity: a determination of how quickly an investor can buy and sell an asset.

Mill: in property assessing terms, one-one thousandth of the total value of the property.

Multi-Family Real Estate Investing: also called apartment complex real estate investing; properties and buildings with more than one rental space.

Opportunity Cost: the cost of what the investor could be doing with their money or time.

Overhead Costs: start-up capital; overhead costs for multi-family properties are higher because these units must be bought in bulk.

Passive Appreciation: those factors that may increase the value of an asset without the owner having to invest any more capital in the property.

Passive Income: also known as passive investing; refers to cash flow that is managed by little to no effort and is oftentimes automated.

Property Management Company: an entity that manages the investments, or properties, of an investor for them.

Purchase Price: the price of the property not paid for by the down payment.

Rental Property: an investment designed to attract tenants, often called renters, to live in the investor's property.

Return on Investment (ROI): the ratio of net profit and cost of the investment.

Seller Financing: also known as owner financing or purchase-money mortgages; agreement when the seller of the property handles the mortgage process rather than a financial institution doing so on behalf of the purchaser.

Single-Family Real Estate Investing: denotes a type of home fit for a single family.

True Cash Flow: the real amount of cashflow you'll make on a rental property after factoring in all expenses such as mortgage, taxes, insurance, fixed expenses, variable expenses, capital expenses and property management expenses.

Turnover: the number of tenants that come in and out of an investor's properties.

Variable Expenses: expenses that vary from month to month. These are repair and emergency expenses that are unavoidable over the long-term holding of a rental property and should be factored into your monthly expenses whether you use the funds every month or not.

www.ingramcontent.com/pod-product-compliance
Lightning Source LLC
Chambersburg PA
CBHW031430210526
45464CB00005B/2132

FOUNDATIONS OF MARKETING: YOUR HANDBOOK TO NAVIGATE THE MARKETING LANDSCAPE

Written By: NATASHA ABLE

Embark on your marketing journey with the **'Foundations of Marketing Handbook,'** a comprehensive guide designed for students, professionals, and inquisitive minds seeking a solid understanding of marketing essentials.

This concise yet detailed handbook provides a thorough overview of fundamental marketing principles, offering a gateway for those eager to attain a foundational expertise. Tailored to be accessible and informative, this resource covers core concepts, strategies, and insights essential for success in the dynamic field of marketing.

Whether you're a student delving into the world of business or a professional expanding your skill set, this handbook serves as the perfect starting point, laying the groundwork for further exploration and practical application.

Uncover the building blocks of effective marketing and empower yourself with the knowledge needed to navigate this exciting realm with confidence.